CW00921558

"With this new book, *The Psychology of Honor* Dr. Roxanne Khan has provided an extraor‹ fields dedicated to understanding and preventi‹ the book will appeal not just to students an‹ ...‹.‹‹is, but also to those dedicated to providing aid to victims of 'honor' abuse and violence, including public policy analysts, health care professionals, social workers, and clinicians."

Todd K. Shackelford, *Distinguished Professor and Chair of Psychology, Oakland University, USA; and Editor-in-Chief,* Springer Nature Encyclopedia of Domestic Violence

"A comprehensive and compelling journey through the dark side of honor, where the victims are sacrificed for misconstrued tradition perpetuated by patriarchy and misogyny. You won't believe how deep it goes till you read this."

Nazir Afzal OBE, *Former Chief Crown Prosecutor and Chief Executive of the Association of Police and Crime Commissioners; Chancellor of the University of Manchester, UK*

"Dr Khan meticulously dissects the intricate dynamics underlying the pervasive issue of 'honor'-based abuses, drawing from intersectional perspectives to provide a comprehensive understanding of how and why violence occurs. Her work showcases immense clarity and depth and equips readers with the knowledge and insight needed to confront and dismantle the structures perpetuating abuse. This book is a vital resource for advocates, scholars, and anyone committed to eradicating honour-based abuse and protecting survivors."

Charlotte Proudman, *PhD, Award-winning Family Law Barrister, University of Cambridge Academic, UK*

"Dr Khan has achieved several significant breakthroughs in this volume: she has addressed the much-neglected area of 'honor' killings in a thoughtful and comprehensive way, she has challenged the profession of forensic psychology for the shameful lack of work in this area historically and she has developed innovative practice by offering the first theoretical model of 'honor' abuse perpetration. I recommend this work wholeheartedly."

Lawrence Jones, *Head of Clinical & Forensic Psychology Services, Rampton Hospital, UK, HCPC Registered and BPS Chartered Consultant Clinical and Forensic Psychologist, Honorary Clinical Associate Professor, University of Nottingham, School of Medicine*

"This book is a must-read for anyone working within the domestic abuse sector. I wish it had been written years ago."

Meena Kumari, *Independent Domestic Violence Advocate and Trainer, H.O.P.E. Network, UK*

"Dr Khan, in this excellent book challenges our profession about how and why we have allowed 'gaps' to emerge in our knowledge and practice. It is essential reading for those seeking to enter practice or research in forensic psychology. It is especially challenging to those of us already in the profession, as it is us who have 'allowed' these 'gaps' to exist and to persist. This book is a call to action for our profession."

Professor Nicola Bowes, *Chair of the British Psychological Society, Division of Forensic Psychology, UK*

"As a pressing global issue, 'honor'-based abuse demands comprehensive understanding and effective strategies for intervention. In this book Dr Khan delves deep into the complexities of 'honor'-based abuse, she navigates through the cultural, social, and psychological underpinnings of 'honor'-based abuse, its survivors and perpetrators, shedding light on its multifaceted nature whilst emphasizing the urgent need for cultural sensitivity, providing invaluable insights for academics, practitioners, and policymakers alike."

Louise Almond, *Professor of Investigative and Forensic Psychology, University of Liverpool, UK*

"At last! A necessary and welcome text uncloaking the true nature of 'honor' abuse–a distinct form of family violence and child abuse that has otherwise remained neglected by forensic psychology. Providing a brilliantly readable exploration of the individual, family, and cultural complexities inherent in 'honor' based offending, this vital resource will equip psychology trainees and practitioners, plus other social and criminal justice professionals, with perspective-changing and empowering knowledge."

Kerry Daynes, *Consultant & Forensic Psychologist, UK, Author of* The Dark Side of the Mind: True Stories from My Life as a Forensic Psychologist, *and* What Lies Buried: A Forensic Psychologist's True Stories of Madness, the Bad, and the Misunderstood

"Dr. Khan's illuminating book traverses awkward terrain in a multidisciplinary manner, rupturing current views and racial bias in the interlinked fields of criminology and forensic psychology. In evoking thought-provoking understandings of a delicate but terrible 'honor' that our world grapples with, this book is a beacon to heal, inspire, instruct, and facilitate."

Edwina Pio ONZM, *Professor Emeritus of Diversity, Auckland,*
Aotearoa, New Zealand

"From a lawyer specialising in 'honor' based violence, Dr Khan's book will now become 'a go to' for professionals working in this area. It achieves the difficult task of highlighting, and at the same time, educating about so-called 'honor' based violence."

Imran Khodabocus, *Solicitor, Head of Department (Domestic Abuse)*
at the Family Law Company, UK, Member of the
Law Society's Family Law Panel and Children Law Panel

"Delving into the complexities of 'honor'-based violence, this multi-disciplinary masterpiece offers invaluable insights crucial for students, professionals, and practitioners alike. With its insightful analysis and practical insights, it serves as an invaluable resource for understanding and combating this pressing societal issue."

Carlijn van Baak, *MA, LLM; PhD Candidate,*
Netherlands Institute for the Study of Crime and Law Enforcement,
Faculty of Social and Behavioural Sciences,
University of Amsterdam, Netherlands

"Very rarely does one come across a scholar and practitioner who addresses the issue of 'honor'-based abuse in such a measured and comprehensible manner. Dr Khan possesses the unique ability to holistically and meticulously uncover the complexities surrounding 'honor,' in a way that encourages readers to reflect and take action. This timely and pioneering contribution from Dr Khan is a must read for policy professionals and practitioners across the board."

Maryyum Mehmood, *PhD, Academic, Socio-political Analyst,*
and Practitioner in Domestic Abuse and Marginalised Communities, UK

"This first book on the forensic psychology of 'honor' based abuse is a must-read for professionals and students alike. It provides a much-needed comprehensive and nuanced understanding of this often misunderstood and overlooked topic. Vitally, by challenging prior misplaced Eurocentric framing and instead centring an understanding of minoritised racial and ethnic identities, this book will help improve responses to these cases."

Diana Nammi, *Founder and Executive Director of IKWRO—Women's*
Rights Organisation

"Dr Khan encapsulates teaching, research, and practice-based knowledge for anyone seeking to deepen their understanding of the complexities surrounding diversity and inclusion in psychology. Her insightful analysis sheds light on the often-overlooked gaps in mainstream discourse, particularly the absence of diverse perspectives. Through meticulous research and a common-sense approach, this book offers valuable insights into the dynamics of 'honor'-based abuse, providing crucial context for both victims and perpetrators. Concisely written with a thorough understanding and comprehensive approach, this book is a must-read for anyone committed to promoting equality and combating injustice for victims of 'honor'-based abuse, Dr Khan has worked tirelessly to highlight disparity for victims of "honor"-based abuse throughout her career, this book captures her expertise, passion and drive for change advocating the rights of victims through her research. Brilliant read!"

Yasmin Khan, *National Advisor to the Welsh Government,*
Founder of Halo Project Charity, UK

"The Psychology of Honor Abuse, Violence, and Killing by Dr Roxanne Khan is a much-needed contribution to the growing body of literature. It is the first textbook to draw from forensic psychology and other related academic disciplines, such as criminology and sociology, to provide a nuanced understanding of "honor"-based crimes. This work explores the micro/macro level approaches to victimization and proposes a new three-phase model for understanding perpetrator motivation and how society responds to these cases. More importantly, it uses real case studies to shed light on the lived experiences of racialized people impacted by the shortcomings of the various systems/professionals (e.g., police) that failed to help. It also provides a comprehensive understanding of the victim-survivor and perpetrator perspectives and calls for cultural awareness and sensitivity to equip professionals with practical intervention strategies. It is a valuable resource for academics, students, practitioners, community members, policymakers, and those working in the criminal legal system with victims and perpetrators of 'honor'-based crimes."

Wendy Aujla, *Criminology Program Advisor and Field Placement Coordinator,*
Department of Sociology, University of Alberta, Canada

"A ground-breaking investigation with real life impact. Dr. Khan provides a crucial missing piece in the way we understand 'honor' abuse, violence and killing."

Shaheen Hashmat, *"Honor" Abuse and Forced Marriage Survivor*
and Former Campaigner, UK, Author of It Ends with Us

"A long-awaited book that every police investigator, prosecutor, specialist criminal and family lawyer, social service and medical professional should reference as a practitioners' bible when dealing with these tragic cases. Never before has there been such an in-depth analysis of the psychology from both a victim and suspect centric approach. In order to present such cases to a judge or jury, this contextual background and narrative must be articulated and understood. Dr Khan's fascinating book will provide a helpful insight and support to all professionals dealing with so-called 'honor' abuse cases. A must read as it certainly challenged my own thinking."

Miss Jaswant K. Narwal, *Chief Crown Prosecutor London North, UK, National Crown Prosecution Service Lead on So-Called Honour Based Abuse, Forced Marriage and FGM*

"A thorough and timely analysis of 'honor'-based violence and its complexities. Dr Khan expertly unpacks this confronting topic with the gravity and sensitivity it commands."

Stephane Shepherd, *PhD, Professor of Forensic Psychology and Criminology, Deakin University, Melbourne, Australia*

The Psychology of Honor Abuse, Violence, and Killings

This important book provides a much-needed exploration and examination of "honor" abuse, violence, and killings from a psychological perspective. Written by a leading authority on the subject, the book draws on a wide range of research and theory on victims and perpetrators to bridge the gap between research and practice.

Presented in two parts, the book begins with a focus on teaching, research, and practice issues in forensic psychology and related criminal justice fields, integral to studying and working with victims and perpetrators of "honor" abuse, violence, and killings. The second part provides an overview of the main issues relevant to the psychology of "honor" abuse, violence, and killings. These include definitions, prevalence, crime characteristics, victims, and perpetrators. The final chapter presents a new explanatory three-phase model of "honor"-based abuse perpetration. Firsthand personal accounts and detailed case studies are interwoven throughout, giving a voice to victims and bringing their real-life stories to the forefront.

As the first psychologically based book to synthesize existing and new knowledge on "honor" abuse, the book is a must-read for anyone working with victims and/or perpetrators of "honor" abuse and domestic violence, including criminal justice professionals, mental health practitioners, policymakers, support agencies, emergency workers, and activists. It is also relevant for any students or researchers of gender-based violence and racially minoritized communities.

Roxanne Khan is a multi-award-winning academic researcher. For over 18 years, she was based at the University of Central Lancashire where she was a Senior Lecturer in Forensic Psychology and led a Forensic Psychology course ranked top in the United Kingdom in a national student survey. Dr. Khan is Founding

Director of HARM—Honour Abuse Research Matrix. HARM is recognized as the first and only global network leading research, policy, and practice on "honor" abuse. As Director of onEvidence, Dr. Khan is an independent chair and author for Domestic Homicide Reviews and Child Safeguarding Practice Reviews, identifying areas of good practice and lessons to be learned.

New Frontiers in Forensic Psychology

Series Editors

Graham Towl is Professor of Forensic Psychology at Durham University and was formerly Chief Psychologist at the Ministry of Justice, UK. He is the recipient of the British Psychological Society Awards for Distinguished Contributions to Professional Practice and forensic academic knowledge.

Tammi Walker is Professor of Forensic Psychology and Principal of St Cuthbert's Society Durham University. She is a Chartered Psychologist and Fellow of the British Psychological Society. Her research interests are gendered interventions for managing self-harm and suicide in prisons, mental health, physical health and addressing sexual violence in universities.

New Frontiers in Forensic Psychology brings together the most contemporary research in core and emerging topics in the field, providing a comprehensive review of new areas of investigation in forensic psychology, and new perspectives on existing topics of enquiry. The series includes original volumes in which the authors are encouraged to explore unchartered territory, make cross-disciplinary evaluations, and where possible break new ground. The series is an essential resource for senior undergraduates, postgraduates, researchers and practitioners across forensic psychology, criminology and social policy.

Risk Assessment in Forensic Practice
David Crighton

Forensic Perspectives on Cybercrime
Human Behaviour and Cybersecurity
John McAlaney, Peter J. Hills and Terri Coles

The Psychology of Honor Abuse, Violence, and Killings
Roxanne Khan

For a complete list of all books in this series, please visit the series page at: https://www.routledge.com/New-Frontiers-in-Forensic-Psychology/book-series/NFFP

The Psychology of Honor Abuse, Violence, and Killings

ROXANNE KHAN

Routledge
Taylor & Francis Group

LONDON AND NEW YORK

Designed cover image: Paul Morris, onEvidence Ltd.

First published 2025
by Routledge
4 Park Square, Milton Park, Abingdon, Oxon OX14 4RN

and by Routledge
605 Third Avenue, New York, NY 10158

Routledge is an imprint of the Taylor & Francis Group, an informa business

© 2025 Roxanne Khan

The right of Roxanne Khan to be identified as author of this work has been
asserted in accordance with sections 77 and 78 of the Copyright, Designs and
Patents Act 1988.

All rights reserved. No part of this book may be reprinted or reproduced or
utilised in any form or by any electronic, mechanical, or other means, now
known or hereafter invented, including photocopying and recording, or in any
information storage or retrieval system, without permission in writing from the
publishers.

Trademark notice: Product or corporate names may be trademarks or registered
trademarks, and are used only for identification and explanation without intent
to infringe.

British Library Cataloguing-in-Publication Data
A catalogue record for this book is available from the British Library

Library of Congress Cataloging-in-Publication Data
Description: Abingdon, Oxon ; New York, NY : Routledge, 2025. |
Series: New frontiers in forensic psychology | Includes bibliographical
references and index. |
Identifiers: LCCN 2024027709 (print) | LCCN 2024027710 (ebook) |
ISBN 9781032290829 (hardback) | ISBN 9781032290812 (paperback) |
ISBN 9781003299950 (ebook)
Subjects: LCSH: Women--Violence against. | Honor killings. | Family violence. |
Honor--Religious aspects.
Classification: LCC HV6250.4.W65 K4827 2025 (print) | LCC HV6250.4.W65
(ebook) | DDC 362.88082--dc23/eng/20240909
LC record available at https://lccn.loc.gov/2024027709
LC ebook record available at https://lccn.loc.gov/2024027710

ISBN: 978-1-032-29082-9 (hbk)
ISBN: 978-1-032-29081-2 (pbk)
ISBN: 978-1-003-29995-0 (ebk)

DOI: 10.4324/9781003299950

Typeset in Avenir and Dante
by SPi Technologies India Pvt Ltd (Straive)

Dedicated to Paul (the wisest man I know) and Mabel (our best friend). Revolute. For seeing the world exactly as it is.

In memory of my courageous mother. For her fearlessness, fierce intellect, and unwavering love. And others like my mother who, with messy hair and a furrowed brow, blazed a trail for their own, and following generations.

Contents

Figures

Tables

Boxes

Foreword

I want to begin by thanking Dr. Roxanne Khan for inviting me to write this Foreword in a book with a subject matter very close to my heart. One I know all too well. As a survivor of "honor" abuse, I have been silenced for as long as I can remember, so opportunities to speak are never ever taken for granted. I am deeply moved each time I can share my thoughts freely.

As the chapters following this Foreword meticulously detail, addressing "honor" abuse, violence, and killings is complex, filled with challenges deeply intertwined with systemic biases and inadequacies. From initial encounters with law enforcement to various professional settings where victims seek support, the failures and shortcomings of the system are very apparent. In this book, you will delve deep into the psychology of "honor" abuse, violence, and killings—a phenomenon as complex as it is devastating. From insidious cultural norms that allow violence to flourish to systemic failures in the criminal justice system, you will confront uncomfortable truths that demand our immediate attention and action.

Regrettably, the tragic "honor" killing of my dear sister, Banaz Mahmod, is recounted in vivid detail and serves as a haunting reminder of the devastating consequences of these failures. The stories contained within these pages are not just statistics or case studies; they are lived experiences of real people whose lives have been forever altered by the impact of "honor" abuse. It is their voices that compel us to listen, to learn, and to act. To truly address "honor" abuse, violence, and killings, we must confront difficult truths head-on. We must acknowledge the pervasive biases and structural inequalities that undermine the safety and well-being of victims from minoritized racial and ethnic communities. This book calls on us to strive for greater diversity, inclusivity, and cultural awareness within our institutions and professional practices. Readers are urged to approach "honor" based abuse with empathy, humility, and a commitment to change. I have been speaking out for five years and passionately calling for cultural awareness and sensitivity—a call that resonates throughout each chapter.

This important book is a crucial step toward understanding and addressing the complex dynamics of "honor" abuse, violence, and killings. It is my hope that by shedding light on systemic failures and biases, we can work collectively toward solutions that save lives and fewer calls for "lessons will be learned."

To the survivors who bravely share their stories, to the advocates tirelessly fighting for justice, and to the scholars dedicated to unraveling the complexities of "honor" abuse, I offer you my deepest gratitude. Your courage, your resilience, and your commitment to change inspire me every day. Together, with open hearts and minds, if we truly want to, we can ensure every person, regardless of race, ethnicity, age, gender, religion, sexual orientation, and disability, can live a life free from "honor" abuse, violence, and killings.

With hope and solidarity,
Payzee Mahmod
Campaigner, IKWRO—Women's Rights Organisation
Survivor of female genital mutilation, child marriage, and forced marriage

Preface

Perhaps the reason you are reading this book is the same reason I wrote it. Each day, we learn that another victim of violence has been injured or murdered, and each week that countless children, women, and men have been abused. Each year, researchers try to count the number of victims of domestic terror. How many people live in fear of intimate partners? How many lives have been damaged, destroyed, or cut short at the hands of a family member? We use these numbers as evidence to illustrate the scope and scale of the problem. We share these statistics with public protection organizations and agencies with the hope that they will intervene. Occasionally, there is a collective gasp as new, unheard of, or unthinkable horrors are reported that stretch our understanding of what is sometimes and arguably termed "civilized humanity."

As a psychologist caught up in this perpetual swirl, I want more than numbers. I want to know why. I want to know how. I want to know why some people are able to cause others harm and suffering. I want to know how people can kill others, seemingly with impunity. I have researched family violence and child abuse for the last quarter of a century. Many of you who, like me, study or work in the criminal justice system know that working with, reading of, and writing about victims of family violence, child abuse, and domestic homicide can consume your thoughts. For many people, this work is a vocation far beyond a career or profession.

However, the more I watched and learned, the more questions I had, many of which I could not find answers to. These unanswered questions began to trouble me. Steadily, the number of unknowns grew and crystallized until they highlighted significant gaps in knowledge about the psychology of victims and perpetrators. With over 20 years of experience teaching, research, and practice under my belt, I was compelled to find answers to these basic queries.

- In the 21st century, why are people with minoritized racial and ethnic identities still excluded from psychology?
- If included, why are their experiences crudely reshaped and forcefully squeezed into paradigms and theories that fail to consider the influence of cultural context on individual differences? In turn, why are their individual differences minimized and cultural context magnified?
- How does this insular approach to understanding human cognition, emotion, and behavior in a social context impact professionals working with victims and perpetrators of family violence, child abuse, and/or domestic homicide in practice settings?
- Do these gulfs in knowledge explain why existing research, theory, response, and interventions for family violence, child abuse, and domestic homicide perpetration are of little use in cases of "honor" abuse, violence, and killings?

This book provided me with a perfect opportunity to explore these questions and challenge the idea that university education and professional training equip students and practitioners to work with victims and perpetrators of "honor" abuse, violence, and killings.

This book—the latest in a series titled *New Frontiers in Forensic Psychology*—draws on key and current knowledge from multiple academic disciplines to present a novel and comprehensive first text on the psychology of "honor" abuse, violence, and killings.

Acknowledgments

My first words of gratitude are to Professor Graham Towl and Professor Tammi Walker—thank you for this opportunity to author what I believe is the first book on this topic. I am also grateful to those involved in the production of this book for continued advice and support—Tori Sharpe, Ceri McLardy, and Annabelle Harris.

Heartfelt thanks to Payzee Mahmod and Shaheen Hashmat, who authored the Preface and Conclusions in this book. I am in awe of their courage in stepping up and speaking out on behalf of others who cannot or dare not speak, and Matt Mahood-Ogston and Concetta Perôt, for their quiet courage and grace under fire. The footprints of their stories run across many pages of this book.

As ever, I am indebted to my husband (and our pup), whose musings (and yops) motivated me to finish this book.

Introduction

This book aims to demystify "honor" abuse, violence, and killings by examining these complex crimes in simple terms. Synthesizing key and current knowledge, this text is written to be intellectually challenging and thought-provoking for university students and practitioners working with victims and perpetrators, whether they have a background in forensic psychology or not. This book also hopes to provide some answers and solace for survivors whose words may be unspoken or voices unheard.

Written as a starting point, this book aims to initiate discussion, encourage debate, and add much-needed nuance to the dominant discourse in family violence, child abuse, and domestic homicide in forensic psychology and related criminal justice fields.

This book is also a call to action to encourage research into victimization and perpetration of "honor" abuse, violence, and killings, giving equal attention to individual differences and cultural context rather than focusing solely on racial, ethnic, and religious identities and differences.

This book has two parts:

- Part one has two chapters. These focus on teaching, research, and practice issues in forensic psychology and related criminal justice fields, integral to studying and working with victims and perpetrators of "honor" abuse, violence, and killings.
- Part two has five chapters. These overview the main issues relevant to the psychology of "honor" abuse, violence, and killings. These include definitions, prevalence rates, crime characteristics, victims, and a new explanatory three-phase model of "honor" abuse perpetration.

Part I

Forensic psychology: teaching, research, and practice

21st-century forensic psychology

WEIRD and "raceless"

Cornflakes, masturbation, and eugenics

Given that the history of psychology is littered with theoretical absurdities and questionable studies, perhaps it is not too peculiar to open this chapter with two anecdotal assumptions. First, that all readers will have either bought, tasted, or at least heard of Kellogg's Cornflakes. The second assumption is that most readers will not know that Dr. John Harvey Kellogg (1852–1943), who, along with his brother, invented the famous breakfast cereal, was arguably the most famous physician of the late 19th and early 20th centuries. Indeed, Kellogg was chief medical officer of the Battle Creek Sanitarium. This world-renowned health resort, owned by the Seventh-day Adventist Church, operated on the Church's health principles that promoted a vegetarian diet, abstinence from alcohol and tobacco, and an exercise regime.

Kellogg also had serious concerns about the occurrence of masturbation in children. He wrote that this "self-abuse" caused children to have a range of ailments. Kellogg advocated parents take steps to "cure the habit" by monitoring girls and boys to catch them masturbating and physically examine their genitalia for evidence and then to shame them. With approval, he stated,

> Bandaging the parts has been practiced with success. Tying the hands is also successful in some cases; but this will not always succeed, for they will often contrive to continue the habit in other ways, as by working the limbs, or lying upon the abdomen. Covering the organs with a cage has been practiced with entire success.

(Kellogg, 1891, pp. 294–295)

DOI: 10.4324/9781003299950-2

For young boys, Kellogg advocated circumcision, to be performed by a surgeon without administering anesthetic. The pain and lingering soreness, he asserted, would be associated with the "idea of punishment." For young girls, he claimed to have found a more permanent solution. He recommended the "application of pure carbolic acid to the clitoris an excellent means of allaying the abnormal excitement, and preventing the recurrence of the practice in those whose willpower has become so weakened that the patient is unable to exercise self-control" (p. 296). In other words, Kellogg, who worked with several American presidents and prominent figures such as Thomas Edison and Henry Ford, was an advocate of female genital mutilation and male circumcision for young children to prevent and punish masturbation.

Nearly 150 years on from Kellogg's writing, female and male circumcision are still commonly practiced, the impact of which can be psychologically traumatic and catastrophic (Junos, 1998; Mulongo et al., 2023). It is noteworthy that Earp (2015) states,

> The non-therapeutic alteration of children's genitals is typically discussed in two separate ethical discourses: one for girls, in which such alteration is conventionally referred to as "female genital mutilation" and one for boys, in which it is conventionally referred to as "male circumcision." The former is typically regarded as objectionable or even barbaric; the latter, benign or beneficial.
>
> (p. 89)

As well as promoting nontherapeutic, anesthetic-free alteration of children's genitals, Kellogg was a vocal and dedicated eugenicist. Eugenics, the scientific and social movement based on Darwin's theories of human evolution, was originally defined as the science of "racial betterment" (Yakushko, 2019). Historians of the American eugenics movement agree that Kellogg's contribution to the foundation of this movement was unparalleled. As the founder of the Race Betterment Foundation, Kellogg advocated practices to improve the genetic makeup of the "human race" by encouraging people with "good pedigrees" to procreate exclusively with those who met his standards of "racial hygiene." And to exclude people and groups whom he deemed to be inferior. For instance, Kellogg discouraged the mixing of races and was in favor of sterilizing people he referred to as "mentally deficient" (Stern, 2016).

How should modern-day scholars and practitioners view Dr John Harvey Kellogg—surgeon, health reformer, and inventor of Cornflakes—and his work? Clearly, it is far beyond the scope of this chapter to explore whether he was a sexual sadist who relished painful operations or if he was simply a product of his time (Gilbert, 1975). What is clear, however, is that his work lived a century beyond his time and that he played a significant role in health reform movements of the 19th and early 20th centuries, influencing American and European societies in a profound way, laying the foundations of many myths not only about "racial hygiene" but also about child and adult sexuality. For instance,

> By the end of the nineteenth century, doctors all over the United States were calling for circumcision to be adopted in practice on males. Female circumcision was less talked about but also gained acceptance, and…was practiced in the United States through the 1950s.
>
> (Loignon, 2019, p. 137)

For males, circumcision remains the most common operation performed on males in the United States (Nabavizadeh et al., 2022), while over 230 million girls and women alive today have undergone this harrowing surgery (UNICEF USA, 2024).

At this point, readers may be wondering what Cornflakes, masturbation, and eugenics have to do with forensic psychology or "honor" abuse, violence, and killings. By way of explanation, the bleak and obscure opening to this chapter is a cautionary reminder that scratching at the surface of modern psychology will unearth unsettling information on the origins of the discipline. Further, much of this occurred in the not-too-distant past and has informed the way current psychology has developed, providing a template for the way the world and its people are viewed today. Yakushko (2019) notes,

> Throughout the history of Western psychology, eugenics has remained a dominant ideological force. Without a doubt, the productions of science that support racist, sexist, xenophobic, homophobic, classist or ableist assumptions have had a profound negative influence on individuals and societies, which are typically central to what brings individuals into psychotherapy.
>
> (p. 10)

In other words, 21st-century psychology stands accused of routinely neglecting structural racism and historical legacies of racism (Hunt & Shepherd, 2023; Trawalter et al., 2020). As a result, the study of human aggression and victimization has been examined almost entirely through the prism of Western academic philosophies.

Ethics, the Monster Study, and other "indefensible" studies

In common with enlightenment in other organized disciplines, the bleak origins of psychology are visible in questionable research studies, some of which were conducted a generation ago while others far more recently.

- The Monster Study (1930s). Twenty-two young orphans recruited to participate in an experiment were labeled as "normal speakers" or "stutterers." Half of the children were praised for the fluency of their speech and received positive speech therapy. The other half were belittled for speech imperfections and given negative speech therapy. Many of the "normal"-speaking orphan children who received negative therapy suffered negative psychological effects, some of whom retained speech problems into adulthood.
- The Aversion Project (1970s and 1980s). In South Africa, during the apartheid years, military doctors tried to "cure" homosexuality in female and male conscripts by forcefully subjecting them to electroshock therapy and chemical castration and to undergo sex-change operations. Most of the 900 abused soldiers were aged between 16 to 24 years old.
- The so-called masturbation article (2020s). A PhD graduate student in England published his findings on masturbating. This "ethnographic method" was used to explore how readers of a subgenre of Japanese manga comics (often featuring drawn images of young boys in sexually explicit situations) think about and experience sexual desire.

To redress the detrimental impact of these studies, professional bodies have issued public apologies for "past wrongdoings," universities have made settlements to participants, with sentiments expressing "regret" over "indefensible" studies, and journals have retracted articles that caused wide-scale "moral offense" (Kaplan, 2004; Reynolds, 2003; Zucker, 2023).

Forensic psychology studies have also been widely condemned despite receiving favorable ethics reviews. Consider an early evaluation study of psychopathy by esteemed scholars Rice, Harris, and Cormier (1992), in which

> [t]he treatment program was so harrowing that a class lawsuit was raised against the institution and its practitioners in 2000. In May 2017, a Canadian judge ruled in favor of the plaintiffs, comparing the alleged treatment to torture. … The details of the lawsuit confirmed widespread denigrating treatment procedures, such as chaining nude patients together for up to two weeks, keeping patients locked up in windowless rooms, feeding

patients liquid food through tubes in the wall, experimenting with hallucinogens and delirium-producing drugs, and a complete disrespect and rejection of patient rights.

(Larsen, 2019, p. 253)

The many disturbing aspects of this study are detailed in a bestselling book, *The Psychopath Test: A Journey Through the Madness Industry*. The author of this book (Ronson, 2011, Chapter 3) bluntly questions the

alarming world of globe-trotting experts, forensic psychologists, criminal profilers, traveling the planet armed with nothing much more than a Certificate of Attendance... [who] might have influence inside parole hearings, death penalty hearings, serial-killer incident rooms, and on and on.

(Ronson, 2017)

The purpose of raising these points is to emphasize the importance of research integrity. To echo the mantra of many a university psychology tutor, research integrity in the study of human behavior requires, at its core, an observation of key principles—ethics, reliability, validity, and generalizability. Herein lies a significant problem regarding the topic of this book: despite the sheer volume of research on family violence, child abuse, and domestic homicide, very little of this has been conducted on or applies to "honor" abuse, violence, and killings. While there is an abundance of criminological and sociological literature on this topic, much of it is theoretical or qualitative and does not analytically examine the psychology of victims and perpetrators. The lack of ethical, reliable, valid, and generalizable research on this topic has had a profound impact on professional practice with victims and perpetrators, which, so it reads: "perpetrators, which often relies on unquantifiable knowledge." In common with the study of psychopathy—one of the most studied and recognized diagnoses in mental health research—much of what is commonly known about "honor" abuse, violence, and killings has been muddied and diluted by popular culture and unscientific anecdotes. To understand the psychology of "honor" abuse, violence, and killings requires untangling empirically based "fact" from media-embellished "fiction" to reliably understand victimization and perpetration.

How can the difference in psychology, criminology, and sociology research on "honor" abuse, violence, and killings be explained? One view is that most published psychology studies (including those on family violence, child abuse, and domestic homicide) have been conducted by Western academics of European heritage in the United States. For instance, an analysis of six premier American Psychological Association (APA) journals found that journal contributors, samples, and editorial leaders were predominantly American, "who comprise less than 5% of the world demographic living in conditions that differ vastly different from the rest of the world" (Arnett, 2016, p. 115). A more recent analysis of the same journals (between 2014 and 2018) indicated still only 11% of the world's population was represented in these top-tier psychology journals (Thalmayer et al., 2021). Despite APA (2023) guidelines and policies on how to include race, ethnicity, and culture in research, theory, and practice, most psychology studies use approaches and measures developed with participants who are mostly WEIRD—Western, Educated, Industrialized, Rich, and Democratic—despite the fact most people are not WEIRD (Atari & Henrich, 2023).

WEIRD psychology—"womanless" and "raceless"

The term "ivory tower" is used to describe a metaphorical place of blissful seclusion. One where people can disconnect from the rest of the world and its practical concerns to pursue intellectual and esoteric interests. Unsurprisingly, this term is often applied to universities and concerns about the research produced by its academics. Care and Kim (2018) consider ivory tower research a challenge for modern education, as "many universities focus on publishing scholarly and incomprehensible academic articles that will only be read by a select few. How do we accelerate the learnings from academic research and demonstrate their usefulness in the real world?" One enduring contradiction of ivory tower research is that many modern-day universities operate in a hypercompetitive, hyperspecialized, "publish-or-perish" vacuum, isolated from the diversity of people and communities they are expected to enrich. In modern-day universities, inequalities based on sex/gender and/or race/ethnicity are rife, as it is across academia more broadly. In this hostile environment, female academics, especially those with minoritized racial and ethnic identities, are at risk of "publish-AND-perish" (Amutuhaire, 2022; Weisshaar, 2017).

There is a stark discrepancy between the rich diversity of people in the global public and the white and/or male researchers who dominate the academic sphere, both in research and publishing. Historically and presently, a lack of diversity of people involved in university teaching and research has influenced both the formal curriculum (via the type of knowledge disseminated in student classes) and new knowledge in academic fields and disciplines (via published research). One view is that university-based teams and studies exclude researchers and participants who are not white and/or male, and that psychology is a discipline that is "womanless" and "raceless" (Cundiff, 2012).

The phrase "the system isn't broken; it was designed this way" has been used to explain racial disadvantage in criminal justice (for example, see Jones, 2013). The same sentiment can be applied to Western university systems as a vehicle for teaching a biased formal curriculum to students who are the next generation of professionals (Jackson, 2020). Readers can reflect on their own university education or academic career by answering the self-assessment questions in Box 1.1 and the impact a narrow and blinkered approach may have had on their own experiences as a university student or an academic.

In the late 1980s, the so-called canon wars discussions were the first within the US academy on representation and racial and gender inequities. Mainly in the field of humanities, these discussions centered on the dominance of Euro-centric, male-authored texts. Academic psychology has, too, been dominated by men of Western heritage since modern psychology was formally instituted in the late 19th century and is reflected in those considered influential in the field today. A Google internet search of "influential psychologists" in 2024 provides a list of 17, six of whom are women, and none of whom are Black or Asian. Finding a list of the "founding fathers of psychology" seems to be far easier than listing influential women—the founding mothers of psychology—or academics with minoritized racial and ethnic identities whose work has evolved and advanced the discipline of psychology but without recognition.

Perhaps it is unsurprising that despite social advancements in the status of people with minoritized racial and ethnic identities, they remain excluded from lead roles inside academia's ivory tower. This exclusion has created a template of

---

Box 1.1 Self-assessment: a "womanless" and "raceless" education?

In your own university education or academic career, how many of the following posts or positions are/were occupied by non-white people or non-white women?

- Senior teaching staff who influence the curriculum
- Senior academics who lead funded research projects
- Journal editors and board members with influence on the publication's direction
- Participants in research studies, findings from which are used to represent the general or global public
- Psychology students enrolled in PhD programs or trainee practitioners who, in the future, will influence the culture of university departments or professional practice

human experience formed myopically on the experiences of people of Western heritage, specifically white males (Cundiff, 2012). Another popular view is that the discipline of psychology itself is a product of studies interpreted through the prism of Western male norms and "academia's pervasive white masculinity" (Chakravartty et al., 2018, p. 257).

Returning briefly to Kellogg, eugenics, and Western academic psychology's close links with the "science of racial betterment," in 1851, psychologists pioneered the notion that Black people were subhuman and constructed the label "drapetomania" to define the cause of enslaved Africans making repeated attempts to flee captivity in the United States (Gillborn & Gillborn, 2021). Most psychologists will know of statisticians Karl Pearson and Ronald Fisher, and of their namesakes "Pearson correlation coefficient" and "Fisher information." Less discussed is Pearson's and Fisher's close working relationship with Francis Galton, the half-cousin of Charles Darwin, known as the father of eugenics, and the extent to which their racist political views shaped their work (Clayton, 2020). While these are extreme examples, racially biased views and beliefs remain rampant, insidiously lingering in current day psychology methods and theories on human cognition, emotion, and behavior. Such racially prejudice views have played a large part in propagating race bias in psychological inquiry, where a legacy of eugenics underpins the formulation of research questions, research design, data analysis and interpretation, and conclusion formulation (Hunt & Shepherd, 2023; Woolf & Hulsizer, 2019).

Specific to the topic of this book are concerns about culturalization, where culture is often presented as the sole explanation of "honor" abuse, violence, and killings (Reddy, 2014). Whether intentional or an oversight, the culturalization of psychology research inquiry is troubling. Consider that research on victims and perpetrators of "honor" abuse, violence, and killings almost always focuses on demographic factors, while psychosocial factors are rarely, if ever, investigated. Yet, the opposite is found for other forms of family violence, child abuse, and domestic homicide. In the latter case, an abundance of research has explored a wide range of psychosocial factors, including interpersonal (e.g., rejection), intrapersonal (e.g., self-regulation), biological (e.g., testosterone), disinhibitory behavior (e.g., substance and alcohol misuse), and psychopathology (e.g., personality disorder) in relation to perpetration. It is likely, therefore, explanations for "honor" abuse, violence, and killings are culturized not only because they are more commonly reported in families who are not of Western heritage but also because individual differences and psychosocial explanations are simply not investigated. This view is supported by studies on other forms of family violence, child abuse, or domestic homicide, where it is uncommon, if at all, to explore in detail the influence of participants' ethnicity, race, and religion.

"To put it bluntly, why would white scholars listen?"

The quote in this subheader is a journal reviewer's feedback sent to Chakravartty et al. (2018) for their paper on race and representation in the production of disciplinary knowledge. This reviewer's remark neatly illustrates one of the many challenges of overcoming racial bias in academia—one that requires white academics in Western academia to question the status quo in which they are the main beneficiaries.

Recent years have seen calls to shift academia away from its historical "womanless" and "raceless" origins toward an equitable approach that values cross-cultural and diversity-related understanding, knowledge, and skills. Researchers such as Woolf and Hulsizer (2019, p. 107) emphasize alternate methodologies that come from "collaborators with varying backgrounds, and an understanding of the unique ethical concerns involved in cross-cultural research, individuals can engage in exciting and important research that is both inclusive and reflective of human diversity across the global community."

There are calls to reform Western education to remove bias and to be more inclusive by decolonizing the curriculum. This view is supported by studies that show scholars with minoritized racial and ethnic identities were almost entirely absent in journal publications and while the volume of their work has increased, the gap between citations when compared to white scholars remains (Chakravartty et al., 2018; Ray et al., 2022). Other studies note scientists with minoritized racial and ethnic identities appear on fewer editorial boards and spend more time under review (Liu et al., 2023). A study into racial representation in psychological research examined 26,000 empirical articles published between 1974 and 2018 in prominent academic journals for three major areas of psychology. This showed publications that highlighted race were rare, and when race was discussed, they were authored mostly, and edited almost entirely, by white scholars (Roberts et al., 2020).

Also, in forensic psychology journals, a content analysis of over 1,300 articles published in *Law and Human Behavior* found only 5.3% of these papers had race or ethnicity as a primary variable of interest (Wylie et al., 2018). A content analysis was conducted on the treatment of race and culture in 493 articles published in the following forensic psychology journals between 1998 and 2003:

- *The American Journal of Forensic Psychology*
- *The American Journal of Forensic Psychiatry*
- *Behavioral Sciences and the Law*
- *Criminal Justice and Behavior*
- *Journal of the American Academy of Psychiatry and the Law*
- *Journal of Threat Assessment*
- *Law and Human Behavior*

Just under half of these articles did not mention race or ethnicity at all, while 90% did not explore issues of culture or race to any degree, and in most cases, they used a cultural deprivation paradigm, focusing on cultural deficits or disadvantages present in racial/ethnic minority groups in comparison to white normative groups (Carter & Forsyth, 2007).

Almost 130 years after it was established as a professional organization to represent American psychologists, the APA (2021) released an official apology for being "complicit in contributing to systemic inequities, and [having] hurt many through racism, racial discrimination, and denigration of people of color." This apology aimed to denounce the APA's history and to redress the harms caused, with a commitment to anti-racist psychological practices. Regardless of efforts by the APA and the British Psychology Society (BPS; its counterpart organization in the United Kingdom), psychology as a discipline and forensic psychology as a specialism are a long way off from reaching social equity. A quarter of a way into the new millennium, it is still the norm for "universal" theories developed from WEIRD psychology research to be naively or thoughtlessly applied to racially and culturally diverse people and populations (Atari & Henrich, 2023). And now, a growing number of academics and practitioners are frustrated with a "raceless" psychology mandate: "[P]sychological science must include diverse editors, writers, and participants in the research process precisely because underrepresented psychological scientists might be most willing to examine the experiences of underrepresented groups" (Roberts et al., 2020, p. 1296).

Modern psychology is evolving from the days when eugenics dominated to now, reflecting the views of the baby boomer generation, Generation X, and millennials born between 1946 and 1994. As the time for Generation Z and Generation Alpha is approaching, it is inevitable the next generation of students, academics, and practitioners will have profoundly different worldviews from previous generations, which will change the way human cognition, emotion, and behavior are viewed and studied.

New views for a new world

Human thoughts, emotions, and behaviors are influenced by (and influence) elaborate structures called cultures and societies, which, as they develop, become a shared history. In turn, each person in that culture and society is influenced by (and influences) their history (Henrich, 2020). Throughout time and in each part of the world, people have pushed for their cultures and societies to be structured differently. Be it marginalized people pushing for equal freedoms or rights or the majority who wish to defend or protect their privileges (Saini, 2023). The first two decades into the new millennium have been marked by the exponential growth of cybertechnologies, enabling people to witness in real time the wide-scale disruption devastation caused by economic collapse, COVID-19, genocide, and war. This turbulent era has seen the rise of global movements reflecting the views of a cybergeneration, which has been a catalyst for global human rights movements by men, women, and people of minoritized racial and ethnic identities.

The 2020s have also seen the seismic rise of social media influencers who promote and embody violent hypermasculinity across the "manosphere," revered by millions of boys and young men as positive role models. Spearheaded by self-proclaimed "misogynists," these online and offline communities promote anti-feminism, violent rhetoric toward women, male supremacy, and a hypermasculine ideology that focuses on the "sexual market, women as naturally evil, legitimizing masculinity, oppression of males, and violence" (O'Malley et al., 2022, p. NP4981; Verma & Khurana, 2023).

At the other end of the spectrum, global campaigns highlight the maltreatment of children, women, and people with minoritized racial and ethnic identities, and their experiences in social life, criminal justice systems, and legal processes. The #MeToo global social uprising and awareness campaign against sexual harassment and abuse (Bhattacharyya, 2018). The #BlackLivesMatter movement reignited in 2020 after George Floyd, a Black American man, was murdered by a police officer—this highlighted the racism, racial inequality, and racially motivated brutal violence experienced by Black people, particularly by the police (Lebron, 2023). Movements such as #MeToo and #BlackLivesMatter challenge traditional approaches of Western psychology by highlighting intersecting inequalities of sex/gender and race/ethnicity at the root of conventional theory and practice (Hunt & Shepherd, 2023; Yakushko, 2019). Unlike psychology, criminological approaches have embraced the intersectional framework to explain how people's overlapping social (particularly minoritized) identities, are linked to systems and structures of discrimination, domination, or oppression (Crenshaw, 2013). Only recently, the APA (2017, p. 6) extended its existing multicultural guidelines to acknowledge intersecting identities and the "need to reconsider diversity and multicultural practice within professional psychology at a different period in time, with intersectionality as its primary purview."

To return to the topic of this book, there are vast philosophical and theoretical differences between forensic psychology and criminology in attempts to examine "honor" abuse, violence, and killings. On one hand, there is a substantial and influential body of criminological research in this area, which adopts an intersectional approach to understand the cultural dimensions and universal perspectives of patriarchy and gender inequality (Alam et al., 2023). On the other hand, psychological research on "honor" abuse, violence, and killings is almost entirely absent. The impact of this is a vast chasm between evidence-based research, which, in turn, compromises professional practice with victims and perpetrators of this specific form of family violence, child abuse, and domestic homicide (Khan, 2018). This issue is considered in detail in Chapter 2.

End of chapter reflections

To consider how to use this chapter in your studies, teaching, and research, read the end of chapter reflections in Box 1.2.

Box 1.2 Chapter 1 reflections—putting words into action

Students and researchers
- In the research papers you read, are participants mostly WEIRD?
- If so, do these papers explain what attempts were made to recruit participants with minoritized racial and ethnic identities?
- Were the measures (e.g., questionnaires, interview questions) used to collect data based on a WEIRD sample?
- If the study designed a new measure (e.g., a survey or questionnaire), was this appropriate for all participants, including those with minoritized racial and ethnic identities?
- If your answers to the previous four questions are "no," was this considered in the research paper's discussion? Are these points considered in your own research projects and articles?

Lecturers and course leaders
- Are the contents of your lectures, modules, and programs based entirely on WEIRD reading and research?
- Are the staff on your modules and programs largely "raceless"?
- If your answers to the previous two questions are "yes," consider assessing this deficit as part of a module or program review. Aim to design and deliver a curriculum that includes and values the rich diversity of race, ethnicity, and culture.

References

Alam, A., Khan, R., Graham-Kevan, N. (2023). Family "honor" killings. In T. K. Shackelford (Ed.), *Encyclopedia of Domestic Violence* (pp. 1–4). Springer. https://doi.org/10.1007/978-3-030-85493-5_528-1

American Psychological Association (APA). (2017). *Multicultural Guidelines: An ecological approach to context, identity, and intersectionality.* http://www.apa.org/about/policy/multicultural-guidelines.pdf

American Psychological Association (APA). (2023). *Journal article reporting standards (JARS) race, ethnicity, and culture. information recommended for inclusion in all manuscripts.* https://apastyle.apa.org/jars/race-ethnicity-culture?utm_campaign=apa_publishing&utm_medium=direct_social_media&utm_source=businessdevelopment&utm_content=diversity-inclusion-ecp_jars_rec_twitter_11022023&utm_term=twitter

American Psychological Association (APA). (2021, October 29). *APA apologizes for longstanding contributions to systemic racism.* https://www.apa.org/news/press/releases/2021/10/apology-systemic-racism

Amutuhaire, T. (2022). The reality of the 'Publish or Perish' concept, perspectives from the global south. *Publishing Research Quarterly, 38*(2), 281–294. https://doi.org/10.1007/s12109-022-09879-0

Arnett, J. J. (2016). The neglected 95%: Why American psychology needs to become less American. In A. E. Kazdin (Ed.), *Methodological issues and strategies in clinical research* (pp. 115–132). American Psychological Association. https://doi.org/10.1037/14805-008

Atari, M., & Henrich, J. (2023). Historical psychology. *Current directions in psychological science, 32*(2), 176–183. https://doi.org/10.1177/09637214221149737

Bhattacharyya, R. (2018). #Metoo movement: An awareness campaign. *International Journal of Innovation, Creativity and Change, 3*(4), 1–12.

Care, E., & Kim, H. (2018, January 30). *Commentary. From ivory towers to the classroom: How can we make academic research useful in the real world?* The Brookings Institution. https://www.brookings.edu/articles/from-ivory-towers-to-the-classroom-how-can-we-make-academic-research-useful-in-the-real-world/

Carter, R. T., & Forsyth, J. M. (2007). Examining race and culture in psychology journals: The case of forensic psychology. *Professional Psychology: Research and Practice, 38*(2), 133–142. https://doi.org/10.1037/0735-7028.38.2.133

Chakravartty, P., Kuo, R., Grubbs, V., & McIlwain, C. (2018). #CommunicationSoWhite. *Journal of Communication, 68*(2), 254–266. https://doi.org/10.1093/joc/jqy003

Clayton, A. (2020, October 27). *How eugenics shaped statistics. Exposing the damned lies of three science pioneers.* Nautilus. https://nautil.us/how-eugenics-shaped-statistics-238014/

Crenshaw, K. W. (2013). Mapping the margins: Intersectionality, identity politics, and violence against women of color. In M. A. Fineman (Ed.), *The public nature of private violence* (pp. 93–118). Routledge. https://doi.org/10.4324/9780203060902

Cundiff, J. L. (2012). Is mainstream psychological research "womanless" and "raceless"? An updated analysis. *Sex Roles, 67*, 158–173. https://doi.org/10.1007/s11199-012-0141-7

Earp, B. D. (2015). Female genital mutilation and male circumcision: toward an autonomy-based ethical framework. *Medicolegal and Bioethics, 5*, 89–104. https://doi.org/10.2147/MB.S63709

Gilbert, A. N. (1975). Doctor, patient, and onanist diseases in the nineteenth century. *Journal of the History of Medicine and Allied Sciences, 30*(3), 217–234. https://doi.org/10.1093/jhmas/XXX.3.217

Gillborn, S., & Gillborn, D. (2021). Racism, psychology, and higher education: A response to 'seeking equality of educational outcomes for Black students: A personal account' by Louise Taylor. *The Psychology of Education Review, 45*(2), 23–29. http://pure-oai.bham.ac.uk/ws/files/149345770/Racism_psychology_and_higher_education.pdf

Henrich, J. (2020). *The WEIRDest people in the world: How the West became psychologically peculiar and particularly prosperous.* Penguin UK.

Hunt, J. S., & Shepherd, S. M. (2023). Racial justice in psycholegal research and forensic psychology practice: Current advances and a framework for future progress. *Law and Human Behavior, 47*(1), 1–11. https://doi.org/10.1037/lhb0000526

Jackson, J. M. (2020). Breaking out of the ivory tower: (Re)thinking inclusion of women and scholars of color in the academy. In N. Brown (Ed.), *Me Too Political Science* (pp. 195–203). Routledge.

Jones, C. A. (2013, July 25). *The system isn't broken, it was designed that way: A critical analysis of historical racial disadvantage in the criminal justice system.* Criminal Justice Analysis: Hampton Institute. https://www.hamptonthink.org/read/the-system-isnt-broken-it-was-designed-this-way-a-critical-analysis-of-historical-racial-disadvantage-in-the-criminal-justice-system

Junos, L. (1998). *Bodily integrity for both: the obligation of amnesty international to recognize all forms of genital mutilation of males as human rights violations* (pp. 1–30). Amnesty International Bermuda. http://circumcisionharm.org/images-circharm.org/1998%20AI%20Report-Bodily%20Integrity.pdf

Kaplan, R. M. (2004). Treatment of homosexuality during apartheid: More investigation is needed into the shameful way homosexuality was treated, *BMJ: British Medical Journal, 329*(7480), 1415–1416. https://doi.org/10.1136/bmj.329.7480.1415

Kellogg, J. H. (1891). *Plain facts for old and young: embracing the natural history and hygiene of organic life.* IF Segner & Co. Digital copy: https://books.google.co.uk/books?hl=en&lr=&id=rrZlipwt6OQC&oi=fnd&pg=PA21&dq=Kellogg,+John+H.+Plain+Facts+for+Old+and+Young.&ots=OizO52F4GF&sig=czRx4pi0X8w2TG6Ij51kytevjaE&redir_esc=y#v=onepage&q=Kellogg%2C%20John%20H.%20Plain%20Facts%20for%20Old%20and%20Young.&f=false

Khan, R. (2018). Introduction to the special issue on honour-based abuse, violence, and killings. *Journal of Aggression, Conflict and Peace Research, 10*(4), 237–238. https://doi.org/10.1108/JACPR-10-2018-360

Larsen, R. R. (2019). Psychopathy treatment and the stigma of yesterday's research. *Kennedy Institute of Ethics Journal, 29*(3), 243–272. https://doi.org/10.1353/ken.2019.0024.

Lebron, C. J. (2023). *The making of Black lives matter: A brief history of an idea.* Oxford University Press.

Liu, F., Rahwan, T., & AlShebli, B. (2023). Non-white scientists appear on fewer editorial boards, spend more time under review, and receive fewer citations. *Proceedings of the National Academy of Sciences, 120*(13), e2215324120. https://doi.org/10.1073/pnas.2215324120

Loignon, A. E. (2019). *Cornflakes, God, and circumcision: John Harvey Kellogg and transatlantic health reform* (Doctoral dissertation, The University of Texas at Arlington). https://rc.library.uta.edu/uta-ir/bitstream/handle/10106/29174/LOIGNON-DISSERTATION-2019.pdf

Mulongo, P., Khan, R., McAndrew, S., & McKeown, M. (2023). Female genital mutilation (FGM) trauma and mental health support during the UK lockdown: exploring women's experiences. *Journal of Aggression, Conflict and Peace Research, 15*(3), 221–233. http://dx.doi.org/10.1108/JACPR-05-2022-0712

Nabavizadeh, B., Li, K. D., Hakam, N., Shaw, N. M., Leapman, M. S., & Breyer, B. N. (2022). Incidence of circumcision among insured adults in the United States. *Plos one, 17*(10), e0275207 https://doi.org/10.1371/journal.pone.0275207

O'Malley, R. L., Holt, K., & Holt, T. J. (2022). An exploration of the involuntary celibate (incel) subculture online. *Journal of Interpersonal Violence, 37*(7–8), NP4981–NP5008.

Reddy, R. (2014). Domestic violence or cultural tradition? Approaches to 'Honour Killing' as species and subspecies in English legal practice. In A. K. Gill, C. Strange, & K. Roberts (Eds.) *'Honour' killing and violence* (pp. 22–32). Palgrave Macmillan. https://doi.org/10.1057/9781137289568_2

Reynolds, G. (2003). The stuttering doctor's monster study. In R. Goldfarb (Ed.), *Ethics: A case study from fluency* (pp. 1–12). Plural Publishing.

Rice, M. E., Harris, G. T., & Cormier, C. A. (1992). An evaluation of a maximum-security therapeutic community for psychopaths and other mentally disordered offenders. *Law and Human Behavior, 16*(4), 399–412. https://doi.org/10.1007/BF02352266

Roberts, S. O., Bareket-Shavit, C., Dollins, F. A., Goldie, P. D., & Mortenson, E. (2020). Racial inequality in psychological research: Trends of the past and recommendations for the future. *Perspectives on psychological science, 15*(6), 1295–1309. doi: 10.1177/1745691620927709

Ronson, J. (2011). *The psychopath test: A journey through the madness industry.* Riverhead Books.

Ronson, J. (2017, December 6). *The story of a man who faked insanity.* TEDWeekends: Huffington Post. https://www.huffpost.com/entry/psychopath-test-ted-talk_b_2973423

Saini, A. (2023). *The patriarchs. How men came to rule.* Fourth Estate.

Stern, A. M. (2016). *Eugenic nation: faults and frontiers of better breeding in modern America* (2nd Edition). University of California Press.

Thalmayer, A. G., Toscanelli, C., & Arnett, J. J. (2021). The neglected 95% revisited: Is American psychology becoming less American? *American Psychologist, 76*(1), 116–129. https://doi.org/10.1037/amp0000622

Trawalter, S., Bart-Plange, D. J., & Hoffman, K. M. (2020). A socioecological psychology of racism: Making structures and history more visible. *Current Opinion in Psychology, 32*, 47–51. https://doi.org/10.1016/j.copsyc.2019.06.029

UNICEF USA. (2024, March 8). *Over 230 million girls and women alive today have been subjected to female genital mutilation — UNICEF* [Press release]. https://www.unicefusa.org/press/over-230-million-girls-and-women-alive-today-have-been-subjected-female-genital-mutilation

Verma, R. K., & Khurana, N. V. (2023). Healthy masculinities and the wellbeing of young men and boys. *BMJ, 380*, 385. https://doi.org/10.1136/bmj.p385

Weisshaar, K. (2017). Publish and perish? An assessment of gender gaps in promotion to tenure in academia. *Social Forces, 96*(2), 529–560. https://doi.org/10.1093/sf/sox052

Woolf, L. M., & Hulsizer, M. R. (2019). Infusing diversity into research methods= good science. In S. D. Keith (Ed.), *Cross-cultural psychology: Contemporary themes and perspectives* (pp. 107–127). John Wiley & Sons Ltd. https://doi.org/10.1002/9781119519348.ch6

Wylie, L. E., Hazen, K. P., Hoetger, L. A., Haby, J. A., & Brank, E. M. (2018). Four decades of the journal Law and Human Behavior: A content analysis. *Scientometrics, 115*, 655–693. https://doi.org/10.1007/s11192-018-2685-y

Yakushko, O. (2019). Eugenics and its evolution in the history of western psychology: A critical archival review. *Psychotherapy and Politics International, 17*(2), e1495. https://onlinelibrary.wiley.com/doi/10.1002/ppi.1495

Zucker, K. J. (2023). Introduction to the special section "cancel culture": Its impact on sex/gender teaching, clinical practice, and research and a call for commentaries. *Archives of Sexual Behavior, 52*(1), 17–19. https://doi.org/10.1007/s10508-022-02526-x

Ray, K. S., Zurn, P., Dworkin, J. D., Bassett, D. S., & Resnik, D. B. (2022). Citation bias, diversity, and ethics. *Accountability in Research*, 1–15. https://doi.org/10.1080/08989621.2022.2111257

Working with victims and perpetrators

2

Any discussion about the psychology of "honor" abuse, violence, and killings will involve confronting uncomfortable truths about the criminal justice system. One truism is the many cases in which criminal justice professionals and safeguarding agencies fail to make culturally aware or informed decisions when supporting victims and responding to perpetrators. This is starkly illustrated in the case described in Box 2.1, which outlines the police response to a victim of "honor" abuse and violence who, over a five-month period, reported multiple people were threatening and harming her and her boyfriend.

"People are following me, still they are following me"

These are the words of 20-year-old Banaz Mahmod to the police. Banaz warned, "That's the main reason that I came to the police station. In the future at any time if anything happens to me, it's them" (McVeigh, 2012). Between 2007 and 2013, seven men, including Banaz's father, uncle, three cousins, and another man hired by her family, were charged with murder, conspiracy to kidnap, threats to kill, perverting the course of justice, and/or preventing a lawful and decent burial.

"My life went away when Banaz died. There is no life. The only thing which was keeping me going was the moment to see justice being done for Banaz." These are the words of Rahmat Sulemani, Banaz's boyfriend, who was another "honor" abuse victim in this case. In the ten years after Banaz's murder, Rahmat was forced to assume a secret identity and live under witness protection. In 2016, after two previous attempts, he died by suicide after hanging himself (Goode, 2020).

DOI: 10.4324/9781003299950-3

Box 2.1   UK police response in a case of "honor" abuse and violence

- 4 December 2005. A young woman walks into a police station in London, England, and says her life is in danger. She reports being threatened by family members for leaving her husband and having a boyfriend. They are accusing her of shaming and dishonoring her family and community.
- 5 December 2005. A police officer visits the young woman's family home. She refuses to open the door.
- 12 December 2005. The young woman returns to the police station to deliver a letter, which names the people she says will kill her. This includes members of her family.
- 31 December 2005. The police are called to a café where the young woman is covered in blood. Witnesses describe her as "distraught" and "terrified." She claims her father made her drink alcohol, then tried to kill her, and that an injury to her hand was caused by smashing a window to escape. The interviewing police officer—who later described the young woman as "manipulative" and "melodramatic"—wants to charge her with criminal damage for breaking the window. In the hospital, the young woman describes the events to her boyfriend, who records her disclosure and later hands this to the police.
- 21 January 2006. Three men attempt to abduct the young woman's boyfriend.
- 23 January 2006. The young woman returns to the police station. This time, she reports an attempt to kidnap and kill her boyfriend. She says she will now cooperate in bringing charges against family members.
- 24 January 2006. The young woman is scheduled to return to the police station. She never arrives.
- 25 January 2006. The young woman is reported missing by her boyfriend.
- 28 April 2006. The young woman is found dead in a different city around 200 kilometers away. Her tortured body is found folded in a suitcase buried in a garden.

This case highlights only a sliver of the complexities in the events preceding and following Banaz's tragic death, still one of Britain's most prominent so-called "honor" killings. For instance, Bekhal Mahmod, Banaz's older sister, was the first known woman in British legal history to give evidence against her family in an "honor" killing trial and still lives under witness protection (Mahmod & Siddiqui, 2022). Also, in leading the murder investigation, Detective Chief Inspector Caroline Goode of the Metropolitan Police made legal history by successfully extraditing Banaz's two cousins from Iraq in 2009, where they fled following the murder.

As well as these complexities, this case is also known for multiple and serious failings by the police. For instance, Banaz reported incidents of rape, violence, and death threats to police on five occasions before she was murdered. Still, she did not get the help she needed (Begum, Khan, Brewer, & Hall, 2020). A police investigation after Banaz's death found two police forces had failed her. The Independent Police Complaints Commission (2008) stated:

> Banaz Mahmod was a young woman who lost her life in terrible circumstances. Her murder has been termed an "honour killing"…we have found that Banaz Mahmod was let down by the service she received. There were delays in investigations, poor supervision, a lack of understanding and insensitivity. In relation to what we believe to be the worst failings—the way officers dealt with Ms Mahmod on 31 December 2005—we believe it is entirely appropriate for two officers to face a disciplinary panel.

It was later reported that these two officers, Police Constable Angela Cornes and her supervisory inspector, received "words of advice," the lowest disciplinary sanction, and Cornes was subsequently promoted (*"Honour death" officer promoted*, 2008).

Thoughtless and inadequate responses by individual professionals in the criminal justice system and the organizations they represent are not unique to the mishandling of Banaz's case. There is a wealth of research on inadequate police responses in cases of domestic abuse and family violence in general (Bryce et al., 2016). A growing number of studies also reveal victim dissatisfaction and fear when reporting "honor" abuse to the police (e.g., Aplin, 2019; Aujla, 2020, 2021; Idriss, 2018). What the tragic death of Banaz and police mishandling of her case exemplifies is the multitude of barriers victims of "honor" abuse and violence often navigate to seek support and protection from professional agencies.

A persistent issue reported by victims seeking professional support is a lack of cultural awareness—whether as a result of intentional racism or deep-rooted bias (Aplin, 2019; Begum et al., 2020; Idriss & Abbas, 2010). The lack of cultural awareness in professional training raises serious questions about the ability of practitioners in forensic, clinical, counseling, health, or educational psychology when working with people of minoritized racial and ethnic identities, including victims "honor" abuse and violence (Khan, 2018). Writing about responses to child sexual abuse social work in the United Kingdom, Gilligan and Akhtar (2006, p. 1362) stated, "Many white practitioners certainly seem to see their insufficient understanding of Asian 'culture' as a major difficultly in the delivery of effective services to Asian families." This concern is amplified for practitioners working with perpetrators of this specific form of family violence and child abuse in a forensic context. This brings into question whether professionals in the criminal justice system are taught culturally aware knowledge and training skills to be able to provide racially unbiased care, support, protection, or justice. The lack of cultural awareness in practice settings when working with victims is illustrated in a social media post by Payzee Mahmod, Banaz's younger sister and herself a survivor of "honor" abuse and violence, 13 years after her older sister's tragic death (see Box 2.2).

In this post, Payzee Mahmod, who also authored the Foreword for this book, illustrates the importance of cultural awareness in professional practice—that is, to improve knowledge and to challenge negative and stigmatizing attitudes about people with minoritized racial and ethnic identities (Khan, Khan, Adisa, Kumari, & Allen, 2021). A fundamental way of achieving this is by diversifying the professional workforce that works with victims and perpetrators of all racial and ethnic identities to better represent the diverse people and communities they serve.

Box 2.2 Lack of cultural awareness in practice settings with victims

Payzee @PayzeeMalika 3.59 a.m.—2 August 2019
Talking about Honour Based abuse is extremely difficult.

Especially when you're talking to a stranger and opening up.

What makes it even more difficult is when you're talking to a professional who has no knowledge of Honour Based Abuse.

How can I begin to understand my feelings, come to terms with the past if the professionals I am trying to get help from are not aware of the complexities of Honour Based Abuse?

I've lost count of the times I feel helpless when talking to therapists who make suggestions that make no sense at all, just makes me realise more and more so many do not understand Honour Based Abuse and have no idea how to help victims.

From academia's ivory tower to "raceless" practice settings

Chapter 1 outlined how Western academic psychology has excluded people with minoritized racial and ethnic identities, and their influence on university curricula, teaching, and research. This has created a blueprint of human experience that draws almost exclusively from WEIRD psychology—that is, from people who are Western, Educated, Industrialized, Rich, and Democratic (Atari & Henrich, 2023).

The view of mainstream psychology as myopic (e.g., "womanless" and "raceless"; Cundiff, 2012) is also discussed in Chapter 1, yet it is clear women's contribution to the field has increased over time. The proportion of women who are psychologists in the United States increased from around 12% in the early 1900s, to 57% in 2007 and then 70% in 2019 (Schultz & Schultz, 2011; Yang, 2023). In an international comparison of gender distribution in European psychology, Olos and Hoff (2006, p. 1) found women outnumbered men in all countries examined. Indeed, with a ratio so high over two decades, psychology could be called a "female-dominated profession." The unequal gender ratio also exists in the United Kingdom, where 80% of clinical psychologists and educational psychologists were women (Johnson, Madill, Koutsopoulou, Brown, & Harris, 2020). In the field of forensic psychology, 81% of practitioners registered with the Health and Care Professions Council (HCPC, 2023), who regulate the standards of practitioner psychologists in the United Kingdom, were women.

These figures indicate concerns of psychology as "womanless" can be abated, to some degree at least. Can the same be said about "raceless" psychology in terms of professional practice? It seems not. Consider that 83% of the Division of Forensic Psychology (DFP), the largest network of forensic psychologists in the United Kingdom, were women. Yet 81% of these women were of white ethnic heritage (DFP, personal communication, 11 November 2023). In the United States, Hunt and Shepard (2022) note that forensic psychology, as a subfield, is less racially or ethnically diverse than the American Psychological Association (APA, 2022). Studies show Black and Asian psychologists in the United Kingdom face multiple barriers to participation and progression that white psychologists do not, and they are less likely to progress in a psychology career (Palmer, Schlepper, Hemmings & Crellin, 2021). Further, the psychology workforce population does not reflect the communities they serve, and Black and Asian psychologists face multiple barriers to accessing training as well as navigating psychology professional systems (Ade-Serrano & Nkansa-Dwamena, 2016).

Why is this practitioner data fundamental to the topic of this book? First, only a fraction of professionals have a minoritized racial and ethnic identity. Second, fewer still have been reliably taught about or received training on "honor" abuse, violence, and killings. Therefore, most practitioners will not have the knowledge or cultural awareness to work effectively with victims and perpetrators of this specific form of family violence and child abuse (Khan, 2018). This "raceless" context has been linked with biases in related areas of professional practice, such as forensic science. Chaussée, Winter, and Ayres (2022, p. 795) discuss how

> forensic higher education…in the UK and the US has pushed for greater diversity and awareness in portraying stakeholders and agents within the criminal justice system. Progress has been made employing a diversity framework encouraging greater consciousness in visual depictions of crime, breaking down racial and gendered stereotypes in case selections, and highlighting the realities of institutional racism in the criminal justice system.

Similarly, Dror and Murrie (2018, p. 19) highlight biases in forensic psychology related to crime details or criminal stereotypes are a threat to objective evaluations: "Biases related to race…and religion have, to our knowledge, never been explored among forensic evaluators. This research gap is striking, considering that these potential biases are such a popular foci of other types of psychological research."

When connecting racial bias, the lack of research on racial biasability, and the eugenic origins of psychology described in Chapter 1, it is unsurprising that Bergkamp, McIntyre, and Hauser (2023, p. 233) suggest there are "areas of incompatibility, or tension, between the tenets of forensic psychology and cultural competency" that equate to "potential philosophical conflicts."

This view highlights the need to discuss this philosophical conflict. Without this dialogue, the one-size-fits-all approach to professional practice developed from WEIRD psychology will continue to limit practitioners' abilities when working with victims and perpetrators of "honor" abuse and violence as a form of abuse that mostly affects people with minoritized racial and ethnic identities.

Challenging bias in the forensic context

Consider this seldom-challenged paradox. While people of minoritized racial and ethnic identities are overrepresented in the Western populations served by forensic psychologists, a vast majority of forensic psychologists do not have minoritized racial and ethnic identities. This anomaly is starkly illustrated in data that shows the disproportionate number of Black restricted patients in highly secure or psychiatric hospitals. Table 2.1 shows in 2021, 16% of these patients were Black or Black British, despite only making up 3% of the general population (Davies, 2022).

The disproportionate number of people with minoritized racial and ethnic identities in prison is common across Western countries. For instance, US data shows Black and Hispanic people made up 38% and 23% of the prison population, respectively (Bronson & Carson, 2019), while comprising only 13% and 19% of the population.

The British Psychology Society (BPS) is the representative body for psychologists and psychology in the United Kingdom. A BPS report found that while students/trainees of all ethnicities were as likely as one another to study psychology at the undergraduate level, of the 17% who applied to clinical psychology training courses, only 9% of Black and Asian applicants were accepted. They were also far less likely to be accepted in more senior National Health Service roles, which was particularly salient for certain religious groups such as Muslims (Palmer et al., 2021). A similar pattern was found for practitioner psychologist data by the HCPC (2023). This showed within each of the seven psychologist strands—clinical, counseling, health, educational, occupational, or sport and exercise—forensic psychologists were one of the least diverse in relation to the number who identified as Black, Asian, or Other ethnic group (see Figure 2.1). As shown in Table 2.2, only

Table 2.1 Restricted patients, prison population, and general population by ethnic group (Davies, 2022)

	Black or Black British	Asian or Asian British	Mixed	Other	White
General population	3	9	2	1	85
Prison	13	8	5	2	72
Restricted patients in hospital	16	7	4	1	68

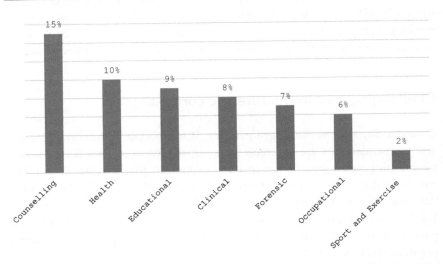

Figure 2.1 Percentage of practitioner psychologists in the United Kingdom registered with the Health and Care Professions Council (HCPC) in 2023 who identified as Black, Asian, or Other ethnic group

Table 2.2 Number and percentage of practitioner psychologists in the United Kingdom registered with the HCPC in 2023 who identified as white, Black, Asian, or other ethnic group

	Counseling	Health	Education	Clinical	Forensic	Occupational	Sport
Recorded Count	3,305	685	4,795	15,810	1,745	1,045	375
Ethnicity							
White	2,495 (75%)	565 (83%)	4,040 (84%)	13,455 (85%)	13,455 (85%)	880 (84%)	350 (93%)
Asian	255 (8%)	40 (6%)	225 (5%)	785 (5%)	65 (4%)	45 (4%)	5 (1%)
Black	110 (3%)	20 (3%)	140 (3%)	190 (1%)	35 (2%)	15 (1%)	5 (1%)
Other	145 (4%)	10 (1%)	65 (1%)	280 (2%)	20 (1%)	15 (1%)	0

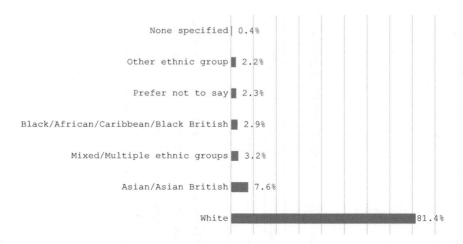

Figure 2.2 Ethnicity recorded by Division of Forensic Psychology (DFP) in 2023 for psychologists in the United Kingdom

100 out of 1745 (6%) practitioner psychologists in the United Kingdom registered as forensic psychologists were Black or Asian.

Ethnicity data from the DFP, the largest network of forensic psychologists in the United Kingdom, paints a similar picture. As shown in Figure 2.2, out of 688 DFP members, around 10.5% were Black or Asian (DFP, personal communication, 11 November 2023).

Studies report that psychologists in the United Kingdom with minoritized racial and ethnic identities suffer multiple barriers and challenges in the profession. Farooq et al. (2022), for example, reported the prevalence of racism, Eurocentrism, and inequality experienced by aspiring clinical psychologists from racially minoritized backgrounds. Within forensic psychology in the United Kingdom specifically, Athwal-Kooner, Ratcliffe, and DaSilva (2022, p. 35) described their lived experiences as three females from Black, Asian, and Minority Ethnic backgrounds working different roles within forensic psychology and that even publishing a chapter on this topic was "a fearful and exposing process."

Overcoming bias when working with victims and perpetrators

While it is understood that 21st-century psychology evolved from ideologies dominant at the time of its inception, much of the current literature and practices in forensic psychology remain almost entirely drawn from Western academic psychology (Atari & Henrich, 2023; Yakushko, 2019). Forensic psychologists, who are largely educated and trained through the prism of WEIRD psychology, conduct evaluations of people with several intersecting identities that differ from their own. How does this discrepancy impact their abilities in professional practice? A survey of 258 forensic mental health professionals in the United States—majority white, heterosexual, women—reported evaluating a diverse set of examinees with caseloads largely comprised of white and Black examinees, with around one in five examinees who were of Hispanic or Latinx ethnicity. They reported significant challenges in conducting culturally informed evaluations, including a lack of (a) appropriate tests for their examinees, (b) guidelines for their evaluations, (c) colleagues from diverse backgrounds, and (d) relevant research (Fanniff, York, Montena, & Bohnsack, 2022).

Such studies reveal problems in applying the dominant Eurocentric models of mental health and psychological distress to people with minoritized racial and ethnic identities. As Western academic psychology has a significant influence on the development of treatments—specifically psychotherapy and counseling—psychologists are exposed to research produced by Western psychology scientists and, thus, are likely to value, "whether explicitly or implicitly, the dominant values of the field, which are often hailed as empirically supported truths" (Yakushko, 2019, p. 2). "Honor" abuse, violence, and killings are complex crimes, and working effectively with victims and perpetrators may involve practitioners from multiple agencies, such as the police, social workers, educators, and healthcare professionals. Studies highlight the impact of racial bias and prejudice in health care and policing, not least because they have "life and death" implications (Alam, Khan, & Graham-Kevan, 2023; Trawalter, Bart-Plange, & Hoffman, 2020). It is also reported that by overlooking important cultural nuances, practitioners who lack cultural awareness have forced a one-size-fits-all approach to safeguarding victims and responding to perpetrators (Khan, 2007). Problems are likely to arise if generalized theories devised from WEIRD academic psychology are forced to accommodate people who are not WEIRD in a range of professional practice settings, a number of which are considered in the following sections.

Forensic settings—risk assessment

Forensic psychologists may conduct research or engage in professional and clinical practice to analyze aspects of human behavior related to the criminal justice system and the legal process. They may review complex case materials to prepare a written report or formal expert testimony, using their expertise to present conclusions to assist a judge or jury in reading an outcome or verdict (Bergkamp et al., 2023).

Despite this, practitioner skills and abilities have been questioned in terms of the ability to conduct reliable and culturally unbiased forensic psychological assessments (Agular, 2020). Without an understanding of multicultural diversity across and within cultures, Dror and Murrie (2018) consider forensic psycho-logical assessments to be "at best unhelpful, and at worst misleading, to the justice system's goals of administering justice with accuracy and equity." With regard to formal risk assessment, Swedish law enforcement has taken a Struc-tured Professional Judgment approach to risk assessment in cases of suspected "honor" abuse, violence, and killings, termed the PATRIARCH (Belfrage, 2005). In the United Kingdom, generic domestic abuse risk assessment tools are used to identify "honor" abuse and violence, such as the Domestic Abuse, Stalking and Harassment, and Honour-Based Violence (DASH) risk identification, assess-ment, and management tool. The many problems inherent in the DASH when applied to "honor" abuse and violence are detailed in relation to police settings in the following paragraph.

Police settings—risk assessment

Despite an increased awareness by police of "honor" abuse, violence, and kill-ings over the last two decades, methods for assessing and managing risk for victims and perpetrators have lagged compared to approaches to other forms of family violence and child abuse. There are concerns about the applicability of the widely used DASH risk identification, assessment, and management tool (Richards, 2009), as it was developed to assess risk in cases of domestic abuse, which are typically committed by an ex- or current intimate partner (Ridley, Almond, Bafouni, & Qassim, 2023; Khan et al., 2015; Payton, 2014).

Reviews of the DASH and its applicability to "honor" abuse and violence have led to the conclusion that, for a multitude of reasons, it is unfit for pur-pose (Aplin, 2019; Turner, Brown & Medina-Ariza, 2022). Miles and Fox (2023) summarized,

> Risk assessment tools for domestic abuse are informed by a wealth of resources, however, the availability of information for HBA [Honor Based Abuse] cases is comparatively sparse. Equally, some of the DASH questions, specifically those relating to conflict over separation and child contact, may be wholly irrelevant in cases of HBA, meaning that the assessment erroneously produces a "standard" (low) risk score. In other words, it is likely that the DASH tool asks the wrong kind of questions for identifying or determining risk in HBA cases, and with the limited generic training on domestic abuse and DASH…officers are ill-equipped to under-take complex risk assessments in cases of HBA. Subsequently, risk assess-ments can fail to accurately capture the specific threats posed by HBA.
>
> (p. 505)

Counseling settings

Psychologists highlight the need for culturally aware theories and interventions in counseling settings for practitioners concerned about issues related to protecting family "honor" and "honor"-based shame. For instance, Ewing (1991) challenged the extent to which psychoanalytic theories were applicable to Pakistani women, as they overlooked the importance of dependency, community, and extended family for many of these women while subjectively overemphasizing the superiority of independence. Overlooking this and forcing existing approaches are likely to worsen these women's situation by increasing their anxiety about breaching codes of honor. A study with health-care professionals in Sweden led to the development of a theoretical model for use with young women anxious about "honor" based family violence (Alizadeh, Hylander, Kocturk, & Törnkvist, 2010). Likewise, a study that explored honor and shame with Canadian Muslim women, focusing on "honor" abuse, domestic abuse, and intergenerational conflict, developed a specific intervention model for use as a counseling tool to help professionals (Helms, 2015).

Health-care settings

As safeguarding is central to health care and social service practice, safeguarding professionals are well-placed to support victims and identify perpetrators of "honor" abuse and violence (Dickson, 2014). In a survey of 233 school nurses across Sweden, over half the respondents reported experiences of "honor" abuse and violence against children (Sundler, Whilson, Darcy, & Larsson, 2021). Specifically, 54% suspected a case of "honor" abuse in a child, 36% met a child who disclosed they were a victim of "honor" abuse, and 36% made a mandatory report of "honor" abuse in a child.

In health-care settings, nurses are often the first to intervene and provide care for victims of abuse and can make referrals to protect victims when "honor" abuse and violence are disclosed or suspected. Due to the many challenges of safeguarding victims of "honor" abuse and violence, studies show creative methods have been effective. For instance, forum theater has been used effectively in clinical training to improve health visitor students' recognition and risk assessment of "honor" abuse and violence (De, Phillips & Moseley, 2023).

National practice guidelines have been developed in the United Kingdom to advise and support frontline practitioners with responsibilities to safeguard children and protect adults from "honor" abuse and forced marriage (Home Office, 2023). The importance of practitioner response is illustrated in national charity data on support service access in the United Kingdom. While over half (57%)

of people at risk of "honor" abuse, violence, and killings visited their doctor in the previous year and one-fifth (19%) attended hospital emergency departments, only 6% of referrals were made by health professionals (Safelives, 2017). Practitioners are encouraged to remember the "One Chance" rule (Box 2.3), which states, "You may only have one chance to speak to a potential victim of HBV or forced marriage and, therefore, only one chance to save a life" (Scottish Government, 2014, p. 9).

Box 2.3 "One chance rule" checklist (Scottish Government, 2014)

You may only have one chance to speak to a potential victim of forced marriage or "honour" based violence; therefore, only one chance to save a life.

- See the victim on their own, even if they are accompanied by others.
- See them immediately in a secure and private place where you will not be overheard.
- Reassure them about confidentiality (in line with your organisation's policy) and explain that you will not give information to their family/friends or community.
- Accept what they say as true.
- Explain all the options to them and their possible outcomes.
- Recognise and respect their wishes.
- Assess the risk they face by conducting a thorough risk assessment.
- Contact, as soon as possible, the lead worker responsible for forced marriage. If appropriate refer to child protection inter-agency guidance; If they are an adult at risk, discuss with your adult support and protection lead and refer to inter-agency guidance.
- Agree a way to contact them safely (for example agree a code word).
- Obtain full details to pass on to the lead worker and record these safely.
- Give them (or help them memorise) your contact details and/or those of a support agency.
- Consider the need for immediate police involvement, protection, and placement away from the family and arrange this if necessary; this includes any action to stop them from being removed from the UK.
- Do everything you can to keep them safe.
- Get immediate advice if you are not sure what to do.

DO NOT

- Send them away or let them leave without a safety plan and follow up arrangements.
- Approach their friends/family or community unless they ask you to do so.
- Approach community leaders for advice.
- Share information with anyone without their express consent (unless there is a risk of immediate harm to them or any children or if they lack capacity to give consent or they are unable to give informed consent).
- Attempt to mediate with the family.

School settings

It is widely reported that truanting from school and withdrawing from education is a potential indicator of "honor" abuse, specifically forced marriage (Britton et al., 2002; Miles & Fox, 2023). Studies conducted in Sweden show other ways in which school settings can be a valuable context for the identification and prevention of "honor" abuse and violence. For instance, it is reported that many of the 1,500 young women in Sweden who sought help from public organizations for "honor" based abuse approached school nurses and counselors (Alizadeh, Törnkvist, & Hylander, 2011). It has been estimated that 10% of girls and 4% of boys aged 15 years who were exposed to "honor" abuse turned to teachers for support (Norberg & Törnsén, 2013). In a study of 4,741 students, a fifth were profoundly affected by "honor" abuse, particularly threats of forced marriage, and had attempted suicide (Jernbro & Landberg, 2018). Swedish school staff—principals, teachers, counselors, nurses—report that despite dealing with issues related to "honor" abuse and violence daily, they perceived it to be unfamiliar and intimidating, and was challenging or threatening to manage (Högdin, Helmersson, & Eriksson, 2023; Lindström, 2020; Norberg & Törnsén, 2013).

End of chapter reflections

To consider how to use this chapter in your studies, teaching, research, and practice, read the end of chapter reflections in Box 2.4.

Box 2.4 Chapter 2 reflections—putting words into action

Practitioners and trainers

- Have you received training to work with victims and perpetrators of family violence, child abuse, and/or domestic homicide, including those with minoritized racial and ethnic identities?
- Have you received professional training in working with victims and perpetrators of so-called "honor" abuse, violence, and/or killing?
- If your answers to any of the previous two questions are "no," aim to work with practitioners who have knowledge and experience in this area to codesign and deliver evidence-based training that is inclusive and recognizes individual differences in people, regardless of their race, ethnicity, and culture.

References

Ade-Serrano, Y., & Nkansa-Dwamena, O. (2016). Guest Editorial—Voicing the uncomfortable: How can we talk about race? *Counselling Psychology Review, 31*(2), 5–9. http://doi.org/10.1007/978-3-030-85493-5_528-1

Alam, A., Khan, R., Graham-Kevan, N. (2023). Family "honor" killings. In T. K. Shackelford (Ed.), *Encyclopedia of domestic violence* (pp.1–4). Cham: Springer. https://doi.org/10.1007/978-3-030-85493-5528-1

Alizadeh, V., Törnkvist, L., & Hylander, I. (2011). Counselling teenage girls on problems related to the 'protection of family honour' from the perspective of school nurses and counsellors. *Health & Social Care in the Community, 19*(5), 476–484. https://doi.org/10.1111/j.1365-2524.2011.00993.x

Alizadeh, V., Hylander, I., Kocturk, T., & Törnkvist, L. (2010). Counselling young immigrant women worried about problems related to the protection of 'family honour'–From the perspective of midwives and counsellors at youth health clinics. *Scandinavian Journal of Caring Sciences, 24*(1), 32–40. https://doi.org/10.1111/j.1471-6712.2009.00681.x

American Psychological Association (APA). (2022). *Data tool: Demographics of the U.S. psychology workforce* [Interactive data tool]. https://www.apa.org/workforce/data-tools/demographics

Agular, R. J. (2020). *Multicultural Research in Forensic Psychology: Where Are We Now?* (Doctoral dissertation, University of Rhode Island). Available from ProQuest One Academic. (2437787875). https://www.proquest.com/dissertations-theses/multicultural-research-forensic-psychology-where/docview/2437787875/se-2

Aplin, R. (2019). *Policing UK honour-based abuse crime.* Springer International Publishing.

Atari, M., & Henrich, J. (2023). Historical psychology. *Current Directions in Psychological Science, 32*(2), 176–183. https://doi.org/10.1177/09637214221149737

Athwal-Kooner, P., Ratcliffe, M., & DaSilva, A. C. (2022). Challenging bias in the forensic context: Lived experiences. In Liell, G. C., Fisher, M. J., & Jones, L. F. (Eds.). *Challenging bias in forensic psychological assessment and testing. Theoretical and practical approaches to working with diverse populations* (pp. 20–35). Routledge.

Aujla, W. (2021). Police understandings of and responses to a complex vignette of "honour"-based crime and forced marriage. *International Journal of Child, Youth and Family Studies*, 12(1), 93–123. https://doi.org/10.18357/ijcyfs121202120085

Aujla, W. (2020). Using a vignette in qualitative research to explore police perspectives of a sensitive topic: "Honor"-based crimes and forced marriages. *International Journal of Qualitative Methods*, 19, 1–10. https://doi.org/10.1177/1609406919898352

Begum, R., Khan, R., Brewer, G., & Hall, B. (2020). "They will keep seeing young women murdered by men. Enough is enough-we have seen too many women lose their lives" lessons for professionals working with victims of 'honour' abuse and violence. *Genealogy*, 4(3), 1–12. https://doi.org/10.3390/genealogy4030069

Belfrage H. (2005). PATRIARCH. Checklist for the assessment of risk for patriarchal violence with honour as motive. *User manual*. Sundsvall Forensic Psychiatric Hospital. Available from http://www.lvn.se/rpk

Bergkamp, J., McIntyre, K. A., & Hauser, M. (2023). An uncomfortable tension: Reconciling the principles of forensic psychology and cultural competency. *Law and Human Behavior*, 47(1), 233–248. https://doi.org/10.1037/lhb0000507

Britton, L., Chatrik, B., Coles, B., Craig, G., Hylton, C., & Mumtaz, S. (2002). *Missing ConneXions: the career dynamics and welfare needs of Black and minority ethnic young people at the margins*. International Specialist Book Services (distributor for Policy Press), 920 NE 58th Ave., Suite 300, Portland, OR 97213-3786.

Bronson, J., & Carson, E. A. (2019, April). *Bureau of Justice Statistics: Prisoners in 2017*. https://bjs.ojp.gov/content/pub/pdf/p17.pdf

Bryce, J., Brooks, M., Robinson, P., Stokes, R., Irving, M., Graham-Kevan, N., ... & Lowe, M. (2016). A qualitative examination of engagement with support services by victims of violent crime. *International Review of Victimology*, 22(3), 239–255. https://doi.org/10.1177/0269758016649050

Chaussée, A. S., Winter, J., & Ayres, P. (2022). Approaches to decolonising forensic curricula. *Science & Justice*, 62(6), 795–804. https://doi.org/10.1016/j.scijus.2022.06.003

Cundiff, J. L. (2012). Is mainstream psychological research "womanless" and "raceless"? An updated analysis. *Sex Roles*, 67, 158–173. https://doi.org/10.1007/s11199-012-0141-7

Davies, M. (2022, May 27). *The over-representation of Black people as restricted patients in secure hospitals*. Nuffield Trust. https://www.nuffieldtrust.org.uk/resource/chart-of-the-week-the-over-representation-of-black-people-as-restricted-patients-in-secure-hospitals

De, D., Phillips, K., & Moseley, M. (2023). Using forum theatre with health visitor students to improve recognition and risk assessment of honour-based violence. *Primary Health Care*, 33(4). http://doi.org/10.7748/phc.2021.e1724

Dickson, P. (2014). Understanding victims of honour-based violence. *Community Practitioner*, 87(7),30–33.https://www.proquest.com/scholarly-journals/understanding-victims-honour-based-violence/docview/1545152274/se-2.

Dror, I. E., & Murrie, D. C. (2018). A hierarchy of expert performance applied to forensic psychological assessments. *Psychology, Public Policy, and Law*, 24(1), 11–23. https://doi.org/10.1037/law0000140

Ewing, K. P. (1991). Can psychoanalytic theories explain the Pakistani woman? Intrapsychic autonomy and interpersonal engagement in the extended family. *Ethos*, 19(2), 131–160.

Fanniff, A. M., York, T. M., Montena, A. L., & Bohnsack, K. (2022). Current practices in incorporating culture into forensic mental health assessment: A survey of practitioners.

International Journal of Forensic Mental Health, 21(2), 146–163. https://doi.org/10.1080/14999013.2021.1952355

Farooq, R., Abuan, B., Griffiths, C., Usman-Dio, F., Kamal, O. J., Toor, P., ... & Yeebo, M. (2022). "I didn't feel as though I fitted in": Critical accounts from aspiring clinical psychologists from racially minoritised backgrounds. *Journal of Critical Psychology, Counselling and Psychotherapy, 22*(3), 6–17.

Gilligan, P., & Akhtar, S. (2006). Cultural barriers to the disclosure of child sexual abuse in Asian communities: Listening to what women say. *British Journal of Social Work, 36*(8), 1361–1377. https://doi.org/10.1093/bjsw/bch309

Goode, C. (2020). *Honour: Achieving justice for Banaz Mahmod*. Oneworld Publications.

Helms, B. L. (2015). Honour and shame in the Canadian Muslim community: Developing culturally sensitive counselling interventions. *Canadian Journal of Counselling and Psychotherapy, 49*(2), 163–184. https://cjc-rcc.ucalgary.ca/article/view/61037

Health and Care Professional Council (HCPC). (2023). *Diversity data: Practitioner psychologists - July 2023*. https://www.hcpc-uk.org/resources/data/2023/diversity-data-practitioner-psychologists-2023/

Högdin, S., Helmersson, S., & Eriksson, H. (2023). Young people in honour-based contexts: negotiations and reasoning on the obligation to report concern among school staff in Sweden. *Nordic Social Work Research*, 1–12. https://doi.org/10.1080/2156857X.2023.2207089

Home Office. (2023). *Multi-agency statutory guidance for dealing with forced marriage and multi-agency practice guidelines: Handling cases of forced marriage*. https://www.gov.uk/government/publications/the-right-to-choose-government-guidance-on-forced-marriage

'Honour death' officer promoted. (2008, December 1). BBC News. http://news.bbc.co.uk/1/hi/england/7758259.stm

Idriss, M. M. (2018). Key agent and survivor recommendations for intervention in honour-based violence in the UK. *International Journal of Comparative and Applied Criminal Justice, 42*(4), 321–339. https://doi.org/10.1080/01924036.2017.1295394

Idriss, M. M., & Abbas, T. (Eds.). (2010). *Honour, violence, women and Islam*. Routledge.

Independent Police Complaints Commission. (2008, April 2). *IPCC Concludes Investigation into MPS and West Midlands Police Dealings with Banaz Mahmod* [News Release]. https://webarchive.nationalarchives.gov.uk/ukgwa/20090104222829/http:/nds.coi.gov.uk/content/detail.asp?NewsAreaID=2&ReleaseID=364298

Jernbro, C., & Landberg, Å. (2018). *Det är mitt liv!: om sambandet mellan barnmisshandel och att inte få välja sin framtida partner*. Stiftelsen https://www.hedersfortryck.se/wp-content/uploads/Det_ar_mitt_liv_Webbversion.pdf

Johnson, J., Madill, A., Koutsopoulou, G. Z., Brown, C., & Harris, R. (2020, July 24). Tackling gender imbalance in psychology. *The British Psychological Society*. https://www.bps.org.uk/psychologist/tackling-gender-imbalance-psychology

Khan, Y., Khan, R., Adisa, O., Kumari, M., & Allen, K. (2021). *'Honour' abuse, violence, and forced marriage in the UK. Police cases (incidents and charges) and specialised training: 2018 and 2019*. Honour Abuse Research Matrix (HARM). https://clok.uclan.ac.uk/36438/1/%27Honour%27%20abuse%20violence%20and%20forced%20marriage%20in%20the%20UK%20%282021%29.pdf

Khan, R. (2018). Introduction to the special issue on honour-based abuse, violence, and killings. *Journal of Aggression, Conflict and Peace Research, 10*(4), 237–238. https://doi.org/10.1108/JACPR-10-2018-360

Khan, R., Willan, V. J., Lowe, M., Robinson, P., Brooks, M., Irving, M., ... & Bryce, J. (2015). Assessing victim risk in cases of violent crime. *Safer Communities, 14*(4), 203–211. https://doi.org/10.1108/SC-05-2015-0020

Khan, R. (2007). Honour-related violence (HRV) in Scotland: A cross-and multi-agency intervention involvement survey. *International Journal of Criminology*, 1–8. https://clok.uclan.ac.uk/13518/1/Khan%20%282007%29%20Honour-Related%20Violence.pdf

Lindström, S. (2020). *Honor-related problems in school. Teachers' strategies and approaches for prevention and identification.* Malmö University: Faculty of Health and Society, Department of Criminology. https://www.diva-portal.org/smash/record.jsf?pid=diva2%3A1486383&dswid=-4613

Mahmod, B. & Siddiqui, H. (2022). *No safe place: Murdered by our father.* Ad Lib Publishers Limited.

McVeigh, T (2012, September 22). 'They're following me': Chilling words of girl who was 'honour' killing victim. *The Guardian.* https://www.theguardian.com/world/2012/sep/22/banaz-mahmod-honour-killing

Miles, C., & Fox, C. (2023). Collaboration, risk and 'just' outcomes: Challenges and opportunities in policing HBA. *Policing and Society*, *33*(5), 501–517. https://doi.org/10.1080/10439463.2022.2147174

Norberg, K. and Törnsén, M. (2013). In the name of honor: Swedish school leaders' experiences of honor-related dilemmas. *Journal of Educational Administration, 51*(6), 855–867. https://doi.org/10.1108/JEA-08-2012-0090

Olos, L., & Hoff, E. H. (2006). Gender ratios in European psychology. *European Psychologist, 11*(1), 1–11. https://doi.org/10.1027/1016-9040.11.1.1

Payton, J. (2014). "Honor," collectivity, and agnation: emerging risk factors in "honor"-based violence. *Journal of Interpersonal Violence, 29*(16), 2863–2883. https://doi.org/10.1177/0886260514527171

Palmer, W., Schlepper, L., Hemmings, N., & Crellin, N. (2021). *The right track participation and progression in psychology career paths.* Nuffield Trust Research report commissioned and supported by the British Psychology Society. https://www.nuffieldtrust.org.uk/sites/default/files/2021-07/1625671007_nuffield-trust-the-right-track-pipeline-of-psychologists-web2.pdf

Richards, L. (2009). Domestic abuse, stalking and harassment and honour based violence (DASH, 2009) risk identification and assessment and management model. *Association of Police Officers (ACPO).* https://reducingtherisk.org.uk/wp-content/uploads/2022/08/DASH-2009.pdf

Ridley, K., Almond, L., Bafouni, N., & Qassim, A. (2023). 'Honour'-based abuse: A descriptive study of survivor, perpetrator, and abuse characteristics. *Journal of Investigative Psychology and Offender Profiling, 20*(1), 19–32. https://doi.org/10.1002/jip.1602

SafeLives. (2017). *Spotlight report #HiddenVictims. Your choice: 'Honour'-based violence, forced marriage and domestic abuse.* https://safelives.org.uk/sites/default/files/resources/Spotlight%20on%20HBV%20and%20forced%20marriage-web.pdf

Schultz, D. P. & Schultz, S. E. (2011). *A history of modern psychology* (10th Ed). Cengage Learning.

Scottish Government. (2014). *Multi-agency practice guidelines: Preventing and responding to forced marriage.* Scottish Government. https://www.gov.scot/binaries/content/documents/govscot/publications/advice-and-guidance/2014/10/forced-marriage-practitioner-guidance-update-2014/documents/multi-agency-practice-guidelines-preventing-responding-forced-marriage-update-2014/multi-agency-practice-guidelines-preventing-responding-forced-marriage-update-2014/govscot%3Adocument/00460555.pdf

Sundler, A. J., Whilson, M., Darcy, L., & Larsson, M. (2021). Swedish school nurses' experiences of child abuse. *The Journal of School Nursing, 37*(3), 176–184. https://doi.org/10.1177/1059840519863843

Trawalter, S., Bart-Plange, D. J., & Hoffman, K. M. (2020). A socioecological psychology of racism: Making structures and history more visible. *Current Opinion in Psychology, 32*, 47–51. https://doi.org/10.1016/j.copsyc.2019.06.029

Turner, E., Brown, G., & Medina-Ariza, J. (2022). Predicting domestic abuse (fairly) and police risk assessment. *Psychosocial Intervention, 31*(3), 145–157. https://doi.org/10.5093/pi2022a11

Yakushko, O. (2019). Eugenics and its evolution in the history of western psychology: A critical archival review. *Psychotherapy and Politics International, 17*(2), e1495. https://doi.org/10.1002/ppi.1495

Yang, J. (2023, November 30). *Percentage of women among active psychologists in the United States from 2007 to 2019*. Statista. https://www.statista.com/statistics/963476/percentage-of-women-among-psychologists-us/

Part II

Understanding "honor" abuse, violence, and killings

Defining "honor" abuse, violence, and killings

3

What is "honor" abuse, violence, and killings?

An important first step in explaining an unfamiliar or complex concept is to provide a clear definition. A definition without ambiguity that lays out connections between components to explain the whole part. One of the main challenges in describing "honor" abuse, violence, and killings in simple terms is a lack of consensus on how they should be defined. Definitions in forensic psychology commonly used to describe family violence, child abuse, and domestic homicide fail to capture many features of "honor" abuse, violence, and killings (Alam, Khan, & Graham-Kevan, 2023). Across academic disciplines, there are numerous, often conflicting views of this distinct form of abuse and murder. It has been described and defined as a crime, a form of interpersonal violence, an act of gender-based violence or violence against women and girls, femicide, a human right's violation, and/or a nonlegal punishment (Cooney, 2019).

Practitioners highlight the need to develop a clear, succinct definition of "honor" abuse, violence, and killings—a working definition that encompasses the range of crime types, victims, and perpetrators likely to be encountered in practice settings (Roberts, Campbell, & Lloyd 2013). In the United Kingdom, differing theoretical views have been merged to develop a working definition of "honor" abuse, violence, and killings for use in research and a range of practice settings.

"Honor" based abuse and forced marriage are two examples of abusive behavior termed *harmful practices*. Other examples are child marriage and female genital mutilation (Khan & Hall, 2020). Currently, without a statutory definition of "honor"-based abuse in the United Kingdom, working definitions

DOI: 10.4324/9781003299950-5

have been provided by the Crown Prosecution Service (2019) and the National Police Chief's Council (2015):

> [A]n incident or crime involving violence, threats of violence, intimidation coercion or abuse (including psychological, physical, sexual, financial or emotional abuse), which has or may have been committed to protect or defend the honour of an individual, family and/or community for alleged or perceived breaches of the family and/or community's code of behaviour. (p. 5)

The UK government defines forced marriage, which is a criminal offense, as

> one or both people do not or cannot consent to the marriage and pressure or abuse is used to force them into the marriage. It is also when anything is done to make someone marry before they turn 18, even if there is no pressure or abuse.

Forced marriage is illegal in the United Kingdom. It is a form of domestic abuse and a serious abuse of human rights. The pressure put on people to marry against their will may be

- physical: for example, threats, physical violence, or sexual violence, or
- emotional and psychological: for example, making someone feel like they are bringing "shame" on their family.

These definitions capture key elements of "honor" abuse, violence, and killings. Specifically, to protect and defend their honor, different types of abuse are committed by one or more people (perpetrators) when they accuse a person or people (victims, most often women and girls) of behavior that has shamed them and damaged their public reputation. It is generally agreed that these features distinctly define "honor" abuse, violence, and killings. What is fiercely debated, however, is the use (or misuse) of the word "honor" in the context of describing the intentional use of abusive behavior to control victims (mostly women and girls) and the use of threats or actual harm if they do not comply.

Minding our language: reframing personalized violence

The use, and misuse, of language to reframe victimization is not restricted to "honor" abuse, violence, and killings. Victim-blaming language is common and pervasive, and it affects some of the most vulnerable people and groups in all human societies. Theoretically, victim-blaming language and views can be explained by the Just World hypothesis, which is rooted in the belief that people get what they deserve (Lerner, 1980). This hypothesis asserts that as most people assume the world to be fair and just, they have a strong desire to see justice served. To maintain this belief in the face of persistent and clear injustice and inequality, many people will intrinsically blame victims for their misfortunes. The view, for example, that as we live in a just world, a person who is being abused must surely have provoked the person abusing them. Likewise, the Defensive Attribution hypothesis (Shaver, 1970) asserts that victim-blaming results from a person's desire to protect themselves from a similar fate, which they achieve by distancing themselves from the victim. For example, when someone hears a woman has been assaulted and this causes them to feel afraid, they manage their fear by questioning the woman—her behavior, appearance, lifestyle—thereby making her responsible for being raped. This reframing makes the victim blameworthy and the rapist less accountable.

Victim blaming enables people to commit, witness, or read about abuse, violence, and killings—either in real life or via any number of media outlets—and to justify or rationalize the distressing realities of a victim's pain and suffering (Khan, 2018). This is illustrated in the following two terms frequently used to describe vulnerable children who undoubtedly suffer extensive forms of physical, sexual, and psychological exploitation and abuse.

- **Child prostitute**. This term is used to define prostitution involving a child and a form of commercial sexual exploitation of children. Similarly, "child sex tourism" is a term used to describe tourism for the purpose of an adult engaging in the prostitution of children. An alternative definition is "the rapist's camouflage" (see Goddard, Bortoli, Saunders, & Tucci, 2005).
- **Child soldier**. This term is used to describe children recruited by armed forces or armed groups via threats, coercion, violence, and abduction. These children are used by warring parties as fighters, cooks, guards, messengers, and many, especially girls, as well as boys, are also subjected to sexual violence (UNICEF, 2021).

Arguments against using victim-blaming terms highlight they are problematic because they infer a choice. Consider the two aforementioned terms, for instance. Children cannot be expected to make informed decisions about being involved in prostitution or armed conflict where they will be exploited and harmed by adults (Goddard et al., 2005). Consider the following two terms, used to describe physical abuse and sexual violence, most often by men against women.

- **Crimes of passion**. This term is often used to describe violent assault or when an act of homicide is not premeditated and is motivated by anger or jealousy. Also described as "murderous love" (see Engel, 2016).
- **Gentleman rapist**. This term is used to describe the "power reassurance rapist" in an established psychology rape-offender typology (see Groth & Birnbaum, 2013).

These two terms describe extreme physical and/or sexual violence using comforting words that sanitize the perpetrator's motives and behavior. These terms romanticize the perpetrator's violent conduct and lessen their accountability. At the same time, the impact of the perpetrator's violence on the victim is minimized.

Coates and Wade (2007) developed an analytical framework to show the power of language use in reframing personalized violence. This framework identified four ways in which people's descriptions of violence lead to inaccurate accounts of the harm caused by perpetrators to victims. First, by obscuring the perpetrator's violence. Second, by masking the perpetrator's responsibility. Third, by concealing the victim's resistance. Fourth, by blaming and pathologizing the victim. When the third element—concealing the victim's resistance to violence—is obscured, the extent of the perpetrator's intention, violence, and brutality is also overlooked. Coates and Wade pressed the importance of language use by professionals in practice settings:

> Key institutions (e.g., education, medicine, law enforcement, criminal justice, …) publicize their ideologies, policies, and objectives as guidelines for social practice. However, it is individuals in specific positions within institutions who must realize these abstract concepts locally through discursive actions in writing and face-to-face conversation. (p. 511)

In other words, each professional and the organizations they represent both play a significant role in understanding the factors that lead to reframing personalized violence and victim blaming. The importance of doing so is illustrated by studies that find violence prevention and safeguarding professionals often do not take victim's accounts of abuse seriously and that victim-blaming attitudes, language, and practices are commonplace (Fast & Richardson Kinewesquao, 2019). In Chapter 2 (Box 2.1), for instance, a police officer described Banaz Mahmod, a victim of "honor" abuse and violence who reported multiple incidents of rape, violence, and death threats, as "manipulative" and "melodramatic" (Begum, Khan, Brewer & Hall, 2020). Studies with police, lawyers, and judges reveal victims have been advised not to provoke an abuser, been derided or ridiculed for staying with an abusive partner, or the abusive relationship is reframed as bidirectional and described as "conflict," "volatile," or "stormy," thereby lessening the perpetrator's accountability (Clark, 2021; Davey, 2016; Goodman-Delahunty & Crehan, 2016). When professionals reframe a perpetrator's abuse and use victim-blaming language, the impact on victims can be devastating and risks revictimizing and retraumatizing them (Graham-Kevan et al., 2015).

Dual identities, "perfect" victims, and "typical" perpetrators

Stereotyped beliefs about victims and perpetrators of personalized violence, and the language used to describe them, have created myths about "perfect" victims and "typical" perpetrators. For instance, a stereotypical view of the "perfect victim" as weak and passive can influence whether observers sympathize with them or blame them (Lewis, Hamilton & Elmore, 2021). Likewise, the use of dual identities based on these stereotypes can influence the extent of victim blame and perpetrator accountability.

With regard to "perfect" victims, studies show dual identities based on race/ethnicity prejudice are linked with the differential treatment of child victims of exploitation. Consider the following two highly publicized court cases of British-born schoolgirls. In one case, Shamima Begum was labeled "monstrous," and in the other case, Rhianan Rudd was labeled "vulnerable" (Jackson, 2022). Shamima, from a Muslim family, left the United Kingdom to join the Islamic State (ISIS) in Syria in early 2015. Ten days later, she married a man almost twice her age and soon after had three children, all of whom died when young. Described in the British press as a "national hate figure" and an "ISIS bride," Shamima's UK citizenship was removed. Her appeals against this, on the basis that she was a child victim of human trafficking and sexual exploitation, were unanimously rejected. In comparison, Rhianan Rudd, an autistic white girl reported to be groomed online by white supremacists, was arrested on terror charges in 2021. Eventually, she was recognized as a victim of exploitation, coercion, and grooming, and prosecution was dropped (Maggs, 2023). Both girls were criminalized. Rhianan, the youngest girl in the United Kingdom to be charged with terror offenses, died by suicide in 2022 (De Simone & Winston, 2023). Shamima remains in a camp controlled by armed guards in northern Syria (Jackson, 2022). The difference is, "with Begum's case, of course, is that she, as a child of Muslim immigrants, could be subject to the racist double punishment of citizenship stripping" (Maggs, 2023, p. 46).

With regard to "typical" perpetrators, studies show that reframing crimes according to a perpetrator's racial and ethnic identity influences how they are viewed and judged. In describing perpetrators of mass violence in the United

States, for instance, Muslims, Arabs, and non-US citizens were more likely to be labeled as "terrorists" while their white US citizen counterparts were more likely to be called "lone wolves" or "mass shooters" (Betus, Kearns, & Lemieux, 2021; Campbell-Obaid & Lacasse, 2023). Media-fueled racialized myths about perpetrators and culturalized reframing of personalized violence are discussed in relation to Problem 3, depicting "dangerous brown men" and Muslim families. Here, it is important to note each of these challenges—the reframing personalized violence, victim and perpetrator myths, and dual identities—contribute to explaining why "honor" abuse, violence, and killings are such contentious terms and contested definitions.

Honor, culture, and violence: a problematic mix

Honor is a powerful word widely understood for its positive connotations. Popular synonyms might include pride, respect, righteousness, esteem, dignity, valor, and honesty. The Bipartite Theory defines honor as having two interlinked components: internal honor and external honor (Stewart, 1994).

- **Internal honor**—a person's self-worth.
  The internal component relates to a person's inner quality and the culture they ascribe to, and thus, is culturally defined. This inner element is a person's integrity or character, consisting of admired characteristics that produce basic self-respect. Having this inner quality motivates people to behave in honorable ways and drives feelings of self-worth and morality (Andersen, 2016).
- **External honor**—how others perceive a person's worth.
  The external component relates to a person's reputation, as others view them—their good name, social position, and value.

Pitt-Rivers (1977) describes the interplay between these two elements:

> Honor is the value of a person in his own eyes, but also in the eyes of his society. It is his estimation of own worth, his claim to pride, but it is also the acknowledgment of that claim, his excellence recognised by society, his right to pride. (p. 1)

Honor is a powerful word because it conveys a powerful human motive. People throughout time and across the world have gone to extreme lengths to defend their own and their family's honor, and the use of aggression to defend honor remains pervasive. Honor is generally understood as a basic human need—a person's need to be recognized within their own social context. Within different societies and cultural contexts, the concept of honor and honor norms have different meanings, which change over time (Björktomta, 2019; Ertürk 2009; Hayes, Freilich, Chermak, 2016).

Although culture is a complex construct, a simplified way to view it is on the individualism–collectivism dimension (Hofstede, 1991). Honor cultures emphasize collectivism, where the value of the group ("we") is higher than the value of an individual ("me"). As the needs and beliefs of "we" surpass those of "me," greater emphasis is placed on protecting the group's collective needs and beliefs. Collectivist honor cultures protect the interests of the group ("we") by encouraging group unity via strong bonds between immediate and extended family, as well as community members. In contrast, individualistic cultures emphasize the rights and concerns of each person ("me"). Where harmony ("we") is a valued trait in collectivistic cultures, personal identity ("me") is promoted in individualistic cultures. These cultural traits are pervasive and influence many aspects of how societies function (Fatehi, Priestley, & Taasoobshirazi, 2020, p. 11). As Figure 3.1 shows, when mapped out by nation, individualistic cultures tend to be found in Western countries such as Australia, Canada, the United Kingdom, and the United States. Collectivistic cultures tend to be found in Asia and North Africa (such as India, Pakistan, Turkey, and Egypt), and also in Europe, including Ireland, Spain, Cyprus, and Greece.

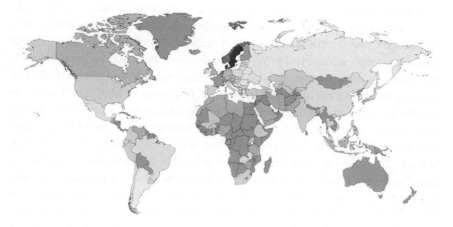

Figure 3.1 Collectivism versus individualism world map

Note: In the original source, the map is in color. Countries colored in green have cultures that are more individualistic than the world average. Countries colored in red have relatively collectivistic cultures

Source: TheCultureDemystifier. Licensed under Creative Commons Attribution-Share Alike 4.0 International license.

As a trait, honor is highly regarded in collectivist cultures. Another prominent feature of collectivist cultures is that they are patriarchal. That is, they are male-dominated and characterized by unequal gender roles. The honor of each individual ("me") and their family and community ("we") is maintained differently by men and women. This is illustrated in Figures 5.1 and 5.2 in Chapter 5. To uphold a good family reputation, men are expected to show strength, be macho, and ensure female relatives act honorably by protecting their chastity. Again, with a focus on their virginity and monogamy, women and girls are expected to behave with modesty and virtue, and to obey their male relatives (Vandello, 2016). As family honor is upheld by a reputable public image, these gender roles are strictly enforced collectively by family members and their wider community. Males benefit most from these gendered codes, as they bring substantial personal and social advantages. Males, therefore, are likely to encourage each other and female relatives to monitor "honorable" gendered codes in their family and community to maintain their privileged position (Vandello & Cohen, 2003). As detailed in Chapter 6, both male and female relatives maintain these honor codes, sometimes using abusive methods, such as coercive control or punishment. In extreme cases, family or community members have killed people, most often women and girls, accused of breaking these gendered codes; that is, they are harmed for acting shamefully and without "honor" (Khan, 2018).

There are several ways in which the word "honor" has been used to conceptualize personalized violence. For instance, acts of male-on-male violence in "cultures of honor" historically reported in the United States are committed to regain lost status and to restore male honor (Hall, Khan, & Eslea, 2023; Nisbett & Cohen, 2018; Thrasher & Handfield, 2018). Notions of masculine honor are deeply entrenched in Western cultures and can play an important role in violence against women in all communities, regardless of their ethnic, cultural, or religious identities (Maher, Segrave, Pickering, & McCulloch, 2005). In the United States and Latin America, when the focus moves from male-on-male violence to a man's use of violence against a woman in defense of his so-called masculine "honor," this has been described as a "crime of passion" (Dietrich & Schuett, 2013). Detailed earlier in this chapter, this romanticized term, used to describe a man's violence against a female partner, lessens his accountability. In Europe, the term "honor" abuse, violence, and killings was used as early as the 1970s to describe a specific form of male-to-female violence against women and girls but was only applied to migrant communities (Yurdakul & Korteweg, 2020). Over the last two decades, this term has been firmly established in Europe and North America, largely due to high-profile criminal prosecutions and convictions. "Honor" abuse, violence, and killings are now intrinsically linked to Middle Eastern, South Asian, and Turkish families, both in countries of origin and internationally, within diasporic communities (Khan, 2018).

Although a variety of terms are used to describe "honor" abuse, violence, and killings, they are used interchangeably. For example, "honor" abuse, "honor" violence, "honor"-based violence, "honor" related violence, so-called honor abuse and killings. Often, the term "honor" is within quote marks to convey that they are someone's words and to highlight the alleged motive of an abuser. The shift from using the term "violence" to using the term "abuse" is in recognition of more subtle harmful behavior, such as coercive behavior and psychological abuse, that plays a large part in controlling victims (Roberts et al., 2013). The different ways in which the word "honor" has been used to define personalized violence and the differing connotations of each have made the definition of "honor" abuse, violence, and killings problematic in three main ways. It is argued that the term (1) implies victim blame, overlooks shame, and has been exploited by perpetrators to justify their abuse of victims; (2) is unnecessary, as it is no different from other forms of family violence, child abuse, and domestic homicide; (3) is ambiguous and has been weaponized to stigmatize Muslim families and communities. For the remainder of the chapter, these three points are considered in detail.

Problem 1: honor (and shame) as a justification

Whichever terms are used, the concept of "honor" abuse, violence, and killings presents an uncomfortable juxtaposition. Most would agree it is an affront to suggest there is honor in intentionally controlling or harming an innocent person, more so because the term was coined to describe the deliberate maltreatment of women and girls by their kin and community when accused of behaving shamefully and without "honor" (Begum et al., 2020). Coupling the word "honor" (universally conceptualized as positive) with plainly negative words such as abuse, violence, and killings has led to fraught debates between researchers, practitioners, and policymakers in academia, criminal justice systems, and public protection (House of Commons, Women and Equalities Committee, 2023). The ongoing debate on this problematic term and definition of "honor" abuse, violence, and killings stems from a need to value victims' perspectives without victim blaming while capturing abusers' motives (Lowe, Khan, Thanzami, Barzy, & Karmaliani, 2018).

Those who oppose using the word "honor" in this context are concerned the term is both an oxymoron and a paradox, leaving it open to misinterpretation. For example, perpetrators have justified abusing a victim by claiming they were forced to do so to protect their family "honor" (Van Baak, Hayes, Freilich, & Chermak, 2018). This is particularly salient when considering Abu-Odeh's (1997) comparative analysis of violence against women in the

Table 3.1 Analysis of violence against women: United States vs. the Arab World (Abu-Odeh, 1997)

Crime	Term use	Term connotation
Honor *Shame*	To **justify** violence against women in the East	• Emphasizes nature of violent act (not the actor) • Violence committed in "self-defense" can be justified
Passion *Excuse*	To **excuse** violence against women in the West	• Violence inflicted is explained without inferring the violent person's character • Violent person (not their actions) can be excused

United States vs. the Arab World, summarized in Table 3.1. This study found "honor" crimes were based on the notion of *justification*. Justification stresses the nature of a violent act (whether it is rightful or not), not the actor. In this way, when violence is claimed to be an act of self-defense, it can be justified. By contrast, in a "crime of passion," a violent person (but not their actions) can be *excused*. In this instance, the harm caused to a victim is explained without inferring what kind of person the harm-doer is: "It appeals to our sense of compassion for human weakness in the face of unexpected, overwhelming circumstances" (Abu-Odeh, 1997, p. 289).

Abu-Odeh (1997, p. 289) also noted an important distinction: [W]hile the West has "passion" the East has "honor," and at the root of honor is shame. A popular view is that the world can be divided into three basic cultural orientations, each defined by their primary social punishment—either shame, guilt, or fear. In shame cultures, fear cultures, and guilt cultures, people respond differently when religiously sanctioned codes are not obeyed (Nida, 1975). There is little evidence to support this theory (Cozens, 2018). However, when results from a web-based survey (the Culture Test; Georges, 2010) are plotted by country, "guilt" maps onto Western European and North American nations, while "shame" maps onto predominantly Eastern nations, as shown in Figure 3.2. There is also an overlap between "shame" (collectivist cultures) and "guilt" (individualistic cultures), as shown in Figure 3.1.

Chapter 6 explores in detail perpetrators' motives for committing "honor" abuse, violence, and killings. Here, it is important to note the overwhelming influence of shame in these crimes. Shame is a profound emotion. It has a significant influence on a person's self-esteem, self-image, self-concept, and body image, as well as their sense of alienation, loneliness, and inferiority (Kaufman, 2004). Shame is often used as a tool to control victims, and it plays a significant role in the perpetration of physical and sexual abuse (Thaggard & Montayre, 2019).

Figure 3.2 Shame, fear, and guilt orientations, according to the culture test
Source: Cozens, 2018.

Distinctly, the desire to be rid of shame is a commonly reported motive of "honor" abuse, violence, and killings. Perpetrators often claim their need to be cleansed of shame overrides their emotional desire to love and protect family members (Begum et al., 2020). In a study of 39 people in Turkey charged with an "honor" killing, Doğan (2014, p. 379) noted there was little expression of shame for the violence they had committed against victims. Instead, they reported they "felt ashamed" because of the victim's behavior. Doğan's view is that justifications for "honor" killings are shaped by cultural influences. Wolfgang (1958) agreed and, in his influential US study, emphasized that perpetrators view the protection of honor as an antecedent for killing, the extent to which they defend the killing as an act that was expected of them.

Another problematic cultural influence related to "honor" abuse, violence, and killings is that some nations have a judicial history of legitimizing these crimes. Critics of this term highlight that in some regions of the world, "honor" based crimes are viewed more leniently in court than comparable crimes, as reflected in prosecution and sentencing. Therefore, when "honor" is used to describe abuse, violence, and killings, this reinforces the idea that in this specific context, these acts can be culturally justified, legitimized, or decriminalized (Terman, 2010). For instance, Italian law was permissive of "honor" killings under certain circumstances, and the Criminal Code provided mitigating circumstances for such killings (De Cristofaro, 2018). A special status was attributed, and if a murder was committed in the name of so-called honor, a reduction was permitted from 24 years in prison to 7 years (Caffaro, Ferraris, & Schmidt, 2014).

Given the prevalence and complexity of these crimes, "culture" alone seems an easy, convenient, and even lazy explanation (Ouis, Staaf, & Cinthio, 2022). As detailed in Chapter 1, there is good reason to be wary when cultural aspects are overemphasized or provided as a sole explanation for complex human behaviors while individual differences are underplayed or entirely overlooked.

Problem 2: "honor" abuse as a distinct form of harm

Some features of "honor" abuse, violence, and killings overlap with other forms of family violence, child abuse, and domestic homicide. It is undeniable, however, that many features make this specific form of abuse distinctive, as detailed in Chapters 3 to 6. It has been proposed that as some of the distinguishable features are politically problematic, "honor" abuse, violence, and killings are best understood in the context of gender-based violence and violence against women and girls, commonly referred to as VAWG. Gender-based violence is universally acknowledged within all societies as a significant human rights violation. Any woman or man can be a victim of gender-based violence, yet women and girls suffer disproportionately (European Institute for Gender Equality, 2021). VAWG is, therefore, an umbrella term that covers the broad range of abuse committed against women and girls. More specifically, any act of "gender-based violence that results in, or is likely to result in, physical, sexual or psychological harm or suffering to women, including threats of such acts, coercion or arbitrary deprivation of liberty, whether occurring in public or in private life" (United Nations General Assembly, 2001). This definition includes domestic abuse and homicide, as well as "honor" abuse, violence, and killings.

Due to the many similarities, some theorists suggest "honor" abuse, violence, and killings are addressed as gender-based violence. A counter view is that failing to recognize the unique circumstances and characteristics of this specific form of personalized violence will act as a barrier to identifying, supporting, and protecting victims. This stance also risks a *criminal and legal* response that is not evidence-based, thereby increasing the risk that perpetrators are not brought to justice and approaches to rehabilitation and intervention are misinformed (Terman, 2010).

Another reason why "honor" abuse, violence, and killings do not fully fit within the VAWG context is that while the overwhelming majority of victims are girls and women, boys and men, too, are victimized. As detailed in Chapter 5, this includes male victims who do not conform to social or gender expectations and/or by association with girls and women who are accused of being "dishonorable" (Lowe, Khan, Thanzami, Barzy, & Karmaliani, 2021).

Despite this, Reddy (2014, p. 28) suggests "honor" abuse, violence, and killings are considered as a subcategory of gender-based violence to avoid "inappropriate focus on the alleged cultural aspects of such violence." This view is validated by an extensive body of research that finds the cultural framing of "honor" abuse, violence, and killings whereby culture is often presented as the sole explanation while other factors are not examined (Reddy, 2014). The cause of this cultural framing is detailed in Chapter 1, while the impact of this is discussed in the following section.

Problem 3: depicting "dangerous brown men" and Muslim families

An extensive body of research indicates a myopic focus on demographic variables, such as race, religion, and culture, has led to the weaponization of this form of abuse to demonize Middle Eastern and South Asian families of Islamic faith (Mattoo & Merrigan, 2021). From this view, singling out "honor" abuse, violence, and killings as a specific form of abuse has created a divisive notion of "us" (non-violent Europeans) and "them" by magnifying cultural differences (Korteweg & Yurdakul, 2009; Montoya & Rolandsen Agustín, 2013; N'eman-Haviv, 2021; Olwan, 2013).

As discussed in Chapter 1, unlike other forms of family violence, child abuse, and domestic homicide, the influence of psychosocial factors is almost entirely excluded from explanations of "honor" abuse, violence, and killings, which instead focus on cultural factors or differences. A point to which Terman (2010, p. 13) asks, "[W]hy are cases of intimate partner violence in Europe or North America never classified as honor killing unless they involve Muslims or Middle Eastern/South Asian immigrants?" One answer to this comes from a systematic content analysis of 500 articles on murder cases in three major newspapers in Canada, labeled either as "honor killings" or "family/spousal murders." Analysis found the former were framed in terms of culture and ethnic background, and as a clash between South Asian/Muslim and Western values (Shier & Shor, 2016). Conversely, articles on "family/spousal murders" focused on the perpetrators' personalities or psychological characteristics, often ignoring factors such as culture, patriarchy, honor, and shame. Shier and Shor (2016) concluded distorted, oversimplified views of "honor" abuse, violence, and killings have created a myth of Middle East and South Asian families as more violent and brutal than Western European families.

These views represent the media's use of reframing personalized violence, "typical" perpetrator myths, and the use of dual identities based on race and religious prejudices. The media is influential in the way it reports all forms of family violence, child abuse, and domestic. With "honor" abuse, violence, and killings specifically, Mattoo and Merrigan (2021, p. 124) considered the use of language in Western media focused on culturalization, such as "Canada's Zero Tolerance for Barbaric Cultural Practices Act (2015), which fanned the flames of xenophobia on a mass level." Further, the influence of "highly mediatized murders" in Western Europe and North America emphasizes cultural differences, specifically that Muslim values are at odds with Western values, thereby stigmatizing Muslim and immigrant communities (Abji & Korteweg, 2021; Terman, 2010).

Altinbaş (2013) proposed that the media seeks to create a moral panic by reporting events by emphasizing the religion of perpetrators if they are Muslim.

Bhattacharyya (2008, p. 89) proposed that Muslim men in general, and South Asian men in particular, have been framed as "dangerous brown men." Due to crude racial hypersexualization, "their masculinity is regarded as excessive and dysfunctional, too absolute in the internalization of restraint, too refusing of desire malleability, too literal in their understanding of ideal masculinity." British academics have also explored the media's portrayal of South Asian men as perpetrators of sexual exploitation and child grooming. Cockbain and Tufail (2020) contend that since 2010, the British media have perpetuated a dangerous, incorrect, and racist narrative about "Muslim grooming gangs" that has dominated popular discourse on child sexual abuse in the United Kingdom. Several academics have criticized disparities in the way South Asian and white offenders are portrayed by the media. For example, in a critical analysis of child sexual exploitation case reports, Miah (2015) found that sexual abuse committed by South Asian offenders was explained in terms of race and culture, whereas their white counterparts' crimes are framed as individual deviance. A significant consequence of this framing is that South Asian victims have been excluded from discussions on child sexual abuse and exploitation, and in part, this is a result of a lack of understanding of the specific barriers they face that Black and white victims might not (Halo Project, 2020).

End of chapter reflections

Language matters. The words and phrases used to define abuse, violence, and murder are important, as they might unknowingly and unwittingly negatively influence the way victims and perpetrators are perceived. This chapter laid out three main ways in which the definitions of "honor" abuse, violence, and killings are considered problematic.

This chapter also highlighted that a lack of clarity in a definition is a problem that can be applied to many forms of family violence, child abuse, and domestic homicide. Indeed, the misuse of language to reframe victimization and victim-blaming language is widespread and affects some of the most vulnerable people and groups in all human societies.

References

Abji, S., & Korteweg, A. C. (2021). "Honour"-based violence and the politics of culture in Canada: Advancing a cultural analysis of multiscalar violence. *International Journal of Child, Youth and Family Studies, 12*(1), 73–92. https://doi.org/10.18357/ijcyfs121202120084

Abu-Odeh, L. (1997). Comparatively speaking: the honor of the east and the passion of the west. *Utah Law Review, 1997*(2), 287–308. https://heinonline.org/HOL/LandingPage?handle=hein.journals/utahlr1997&div=23&id=&page=

Alam, A., Khan, R., Graham-Kevan, N. (2023). Family "honor" killings. In T. K. Shackelford (Ed.), *Encyclopedia of domestic violence* (pp. 1–4). Springer. https://doi.org/10.1007/978-3-030-85493-5_528-1

Altınbaş, N. (2013). honor-related violence in the context of patriarchy, multicultural politics, and Islamophobia after 9/11. *American Journal of Islamic Social Sciences, 30*(3), 1–19.

Andersen, P. T. (2016). After honor. In P. T. Andersen (Ed.), *Story and emotion: A study in affective narratology* (pp. 150–171). Universitetsforlaget. https://doi.org/10.18261/97882150 28255-2016-07

Begum, R., Khan, R., Brewer, G., & Hall, B. (2020). "They will keep seeing young women murdered by men. Enough is enough-we have seen too many women lose their lives". Lessons for professionals working with victims of 'honour' abuse and violence. *Genealogy, 4*(3), 1–12. https://doi.org/10.3390/genealogy4030069

Betus, A. E., Kearns, E. M., & Lemieux, A. F. (2021). How perpetrator identity (sometimes) influences media framing attacks as "terrorism" or "mental illness". *Communication Research, 48*(8), 1133–1156. https://doi.org/10.1177/0093650220971142

Bhattacharyya, G. (2008). *Dangerous brown men*. ZedBooks.

Björktomta, S. B. (2019). Honor-based violence in Sweden–Norms of honor and chastity. *Journal of Family Violence, 34*(5), 449–460. https://doi.org/10.1007/s10896-019-00039-1

Caffaro, F., Ferraris, F., & Schmidt, S. (2014). Gender differences in the perception of honour killing in individualist versus collectivistic cultures: Comparison between Italy and Turkey. *Sex Roles, 71*(9), 296–318. https://doi.org/10.1007/s11199-014-0413-5

Campbell-Obaid, M., & Lacasse, K. (2023). A perpetrator by any other name: Unpacking the characterizations and consequences of the "terrorist," "lone wolf," and "mass shooter" labels for perpetrators of mass violence. *Psychology of Violence, 13*(5), 425–435 https://psycnet.apa.org/doi/10.1037/vio0000476

Clark, V. E. (2021). Victim-blaming discourse underpinning police responses to domestic violence: A critical social work perspective. *Social Work & Policy Studies: Social Justice, Practice and Theory, 4*(1), 1–15. https://openjournals.library.sydney.edu.au/SWPS/article/view/14959

Coates, L., & Wade, A. (2007). Language and violence: Analysis of four discursive operations. *Journal of Family Violence, 22*(7), 511–522. https://doi.org/10.1007/s10896-007-9082-2

Cockbain, E., & Tufail, W. (2020). Failing victims, fuelling hate: Challenging the harms of the 'Muslim grooming gangs' narrative. *Race & Class, 61*(3), 3–32. https://doi.org/10.1177/0306396819895727

Cooney, M. (2019). *Execution by family: A theory of honor violence*. Routledge.

Cozens, S. (2018). Shame cultures, fear cultures, and guilt cultures: Reviewing the evidence. *International Bulletin of Mission Research, 42*(4), 326–336. https://doi.org/10.1177/2396939318764087

Crown Prosecution Service. (2019). *So-called honour-based abuse and forced marriage: Guidance on identifying and flagging cases*. https://www.cps.gov.uk/legal-guidance/so-called-honour-based-abuse-and-forced-marriage-guidance-identifying-and-flagging

De Simone, D. & Winston, A. (2023, January 3). Rhianan Rudd: MI5 had evidence teen terror suspect was exploited. *The Guardian*. https://www.bbc.co.uk/news/uk-63736944

Davey, M. (2016, August 15). Lawyers use victim-blaming language in domestic violence cases, says report. *The Guardian*. https://www.theguardian.com/society/2016/aug/15/lawyers-use-victim-blaming-language-in-domestic-violence-cases-says-report

De Cristofaro, E. (2018). The crime of honor: An Italian story. *Historia et ius, 14*, 1–12. http://www.historiaetius.eu/uploads/5/9/4/8/5948821/14_15_de_cristofaro.pdf

Dietrich, D. M., & Schuett, J. M. (2013). Culture of honor and attitudes toward intimate partner violence in Latinos. *Sage Open, 3*(2), https://doi.org/10.1177/2158244013489685

Doğan, R. (2014). Different cultural understandings of honor that inspire killing: An inquiry into the defendant's perspective. *Homicide Studies, 18*(4), 363–388. https://doi.org/10.1177/1088767914526717

Engel, H. (2016). *Crimes of passion: an unblinking look at murderous love.* Open Road Media.

Ertürk, Y. (2009). Towards a post-patriarchal gender order: Confronting the universality and the particularity of violence against women. *Sociologisk Forskning, 46*(4), 61–70. https://www.jstor.org/stable/20853687

European Institute for Gender Equality. (2021). *What is gender-based violence?* https://eige.europa.eu/gender-based-violence/what-is-gender-based-violence

Fast, E., & Kinewesquao, C. R. (2019). Victim-blaming and the crisis of representation in the violence prevention field. *International Journal of Child, Youth and Family Studies, 10*(1), 3–25. https://doi.org/10.18357/ijcyfs101201918804

Fatehi, K., Priestley, J. L., & Taasoobshirazi, G. (2020). The expanded view of individualism and collectivism: One, two, or four dimensions? *International Journal of Cross Cultural Management, 20*(1), 7–24. https://doi.org/10.1177/1470595820913077

Georges, J. (2010). From shame to honor: a theological reading of Romans for honor-shame contexts. *Missiology, 38*(3), 295–307.

Goddard, C., Bortoli, L. D., Saunders, B. J., & Tucci, J. (2005). The rapist's camouflage: 'Child prostitution'. *Child Abuse Review: Journal of the British Association for the Study and Prevention of Child Abuse and Neglect, 14*(4), 275–291. https://doi.org/10.1002/car.894

Goodman-Delahunty, J. & Crehan, A. (2016). Enhancing police responses to domestic violence incidents: Reports from client advocates in New South Wales. *Violence Against Women, 22*(8), 1007–1026. https://doi.org/10.1177/1077801215613854

Graham-Kevan, N., Brooks, M., Willan, V. J., Lowe, M., Robinson, P., Khan, R., … & Bryce, J. (2015). Repeat victimisation, retraumatisation and victim vulnerability. *The Open Criminology Journal, 8*(1), 36–48. http://doi.org/10.2174/1874917801508010036

Groth, A. N., & Birnbaum, H. J. (2013). *Men who rape: The psychology of the offender.* New York: Springer.

Hall, B., Khan, R. & Eslea, M. (2023). Manhood, in cultures of honor: For social status. In T. K. Shackelford (Ed.), *Springer nature encyclopedia of domestic violence.* Springer. http://doi.org/10.1007/978-3-030-85493-5_2055-1

Halo Project. (2020). *Invisible survivors. The long wait for justice.* Police response to BAME victims of sexual abuse. https://assets.publishing.service.gov.uk/media/602fb7678fa8f5432bc23d92/Invisible_survivors___The_long_wait_for_justice.pdf

Hayes, B. E., Freilich, J. D., & Chermak, S. M. (2016). An exploratory study of honor crimes in the United States. *Journal of Family Violence, 31*(3), 1–12. https://doi.org/10.1007/s10896-016-9801-7

Hofstede, G. (1991). Empirical models of cultural differences. In N. Bleichrodt & P. J. D. Drenth (Eds.), *Contemporary issues in cross-cultural psychology* (pp. 4–20). Swets & Zeitlinger Publishers.

House of Commons, Women and Equalities Committee. (2023, July 19). *So-called honour-based abuse.* https://committees.parliament.uk/publications/40929/documents/200424/default/

Jackson, L. B. (2022). *The monstrous & the vulnerable: Framing British Jihadi brides.* Oxford University Press.

Kaufman, G. (2004). *The psychology of shame: Theory and treatment of shame-based syndromes.* Springer Publishing Company.

Khan, R. & Hall, B. (2020). *Harmful traditional practices in the workplace: Guidance for best practice.* Honour Abuse Research Matrix (HARM). https://clok.uclan.ac.uk/32803/7/32803%20 Harmful%20Traditional%20Practices%20in%20the%20Workplace%20-%20 Guidance%20for%20Best%20Practice%202020.pdf

Khan, R. (2018). Attitudes towards 'honor' violence and killings in collectivist cultures: Gender differences in Middle Eastern, North African, South Asian (MENASA) and Turkish populations. In J. L. Ireland, P. Birch, & C. A. Ireland (Eds.), *International handbook in aggression: Current issues and perspectives* (pp. 216–226). Routledge.

Korteweg, A., & Yurdakul, G. (2009). Islam, gender, and immigrant integration: Boundary drawing in discourses on honour killing in the Netherlands and Germany. *Ethnic and Racial Studies, 32*(2), 218–238. https://doi.org/10.1080/01419870802065218

Lerner, M. J. (1980). *The belief in a just world.* Springer US.

Lewis, J. A., Hamilton, J. C., & Elmore, J. D. (2021). Describing the ideal victim: A linguistic analysis of victim descriptions. *Current Psychology, 40,* 4324–4332. https://doi.org/10.1007/s12144-019-00347-1

Lowe, M., Khan, R., Thanzami, V., Barzy, M., & Karmaliani, R. (2021). anti-gay "honor" abuse: A multinational attitudinal study of collectivist- versus individualist-orientated populations in Asia and England. *Journal of Interpersonal Violence, 36*(15–16), 7866–7885. https://doi.org/10.1177/0886260519838493

Lowe, M., Khan, R., Thanzami, V., Barzy, M., & Karmaliani, R. (2018). Attitudes toward intimate partner "honor"-based violence in India, Iran, Malaysia and Pakistan. *Journal of Aggression, Conflict and Peace Research, 10*(4), 283–292. https://doi.org/10.1108/JACPR-09-2017-0324

Maggs, J. (2023). Not the end of the story. *Socialist Lawyer, 92,* 46–47. https://www.jstor.org/stable/48725086

Maher J. M., Segrave M., Pickering S., McCulloch J. (2005). Honouring white masculinity: Culture, terror, provocation. *Australian Feminist Law Journal, 23,* 147–176. https://doi.org/10.1080/13200968.2005.10854348

Mattoo, D. & Merrigan, S. E. (2021). "Barbaric" cultural practices: Culturalizing violence and the failure to protect women in Canada. *International Journal of Child, Youth and Family Studies, 12*(1), 124–142. https://doi.org/10.18357/ijcyfs121202120086

Miah, S. (2015). The groomers and the question of race. *Identity Papers: A Journal of British and Irish studies, 1*(1), 54–65. https://search.informit.org/doi/abs/10.3316/INFORMIT.642917745109519

Montoya, C., & Rolandsen Agustín, L. (2013). The othering of domestic violence: The EU and cultural framings of violence against women. *Social Politics, 20*(4), 534–557. https://doi.org/10.1093/sp/jxt020

National Police Chiefs' Council. (2015). *Honour based abuse, forced marriage and female genital mutilation: A policing strategy for England, Wales and Northern Ireland – Eradicating honour based abuse, force marriage and female genital mutilation together.* Home Office. https://library.college.police.uk/docs/appref/Final%20NPCC%20HBA%20strategy%20 2015%202018December%202015.pdf

Ne'eman-Haviv, V. (2021). Honor killings in Muslim and Western countries in modern times: A critical literature review and definitional implications. *Journal of Family Theory & Review, 13*(3), 381–397. https://doi.org/10.1111/jftr.12426

Nida, E. A. (1975). *Customs and cultures: Anthropology for Christian missions.* William Carey Library.

Nisbett, R. E. & Cohen, D. (2018). *Culture of honor: The psychology of violence in the South.* Routledge.

Olwan, D. M. (2013). Gendered violence, cultural otherness, and honour crimes in Canadian national logics. *Canadian Journal of Sociology, 38*(4), 533–556. https://www.jstor.org/stable/10.2307/canajsocicahican.38.4.533

Ouis, P., Staaf, A., & Cinthio, H. (2022). "That's how we were raised": Perpetrator perspectives in relation to legislative changes targeting honour related violence in Sweden. *Nordic Journal on Law and Society, 5*(01), 1–33. https://doi.org/10.36368/njolas.v5i01.191

Pitt-Rivers, J. (1977). *The fate of Shechem or the politics of sex: Essays in the anthropology of the Mediterranean.* Cambridge University Press.

Reddy, R. (2014). Domestic violence or cultural tradition? Approaches to 'Honour Killing' as species and subspecies in English legal practice. In A. K. Gill, C. Strange, & K. Roberts (Eds.) *'Honour' killing and violence* (pp. 22–32). Palgrave Macmillan. https://doi.org/10.1057/9781137289568_2

Roberts, K. A., Campbell, G., & Lloyd, G. (2013). *Honor-based violence: Policing and prevention.* CRC Press.

Shaver, K. G. (1970). Defensive attribution: Effects of severity and relevance on the responsibility assigned for an accident. *Journal of Personality and Social Psychology, 14*(2), 101–113. https://doi.org/10.1037/h0028777

Shier, A., & Shor, E. (2016). "Shades of Foreign Evil": "Honor Killings" and "Family Murders" in the Canadian press. *Violence Against Women, 22*(10), 1163–1188. https://doi.org/10.1177/1077801215621176

Stewart, F. H. (1994). *Honor.* Chicago University Press.

Terman, R. L. (2010). To specify or single out: Should we use the term 'honour killing'. *Muslim World Journal of Human Rights, 7*, 1–39. https://doi.org/10.2202/1554-4419.1162

Thaggard, S., & Montayre, J. (2019). "There was no-one I could turn to because I was ashamed": Shame in the narratives of women affected by IPV. *Wome's Studies International Forum, 74*, 218–223. https://doi.org/10.1016/j.wsif.2019.05.005

Thrasher, J., & Handfield, T. (2018). Honor and violence: An account of feuds, duels, and honor killings. *Human Nature, 29*, 371–389. https://doi.org/10.1007/s12110-018-9324-4

UNICEF. (2021). *Children recruited by armed forces or armed groups.* https://www.unicef.org/protection/children-recruited-by-armed-forces

United Nations General Assembly. (2001). *Working towards the elimination of crimes against women committed in the name of honour.* In United Nations Digital Library. https://digitallibrary.un.org/record/428882?ln=en

Van Baak, C., Hayes, B. E., Freilich, J. D., & Chermak, S. M. (2018). Honor crimes in the United States and offenders' neutralization techniques. *Deviant Behavior, 39*(2), 187–202. https://doi.org/10.1080/01639625.2016.1266870

Vandello, J. (2016). Do we need a psychology of women in the Islamic world?. *Sex Roles, 75*, 623–629. https://doi.org/10.1007/s11199-016-0691-1

Vandello, J. A., & Cohen, D. (2003). Male honor and female fidelity: Implicit cultural scripts that perpetuate domestic violence. *Journal of Personality and Social Psychology, 84*(5), 997–1010. https://doi.org/10.1037/0022-3514.84.5.997

Wolfgang, M. E. (1958). *Patterns in criminal homicide.* University of Pennsylvania Press.

Yurdakul, G., & Korteweg, A. C. (2020). State responsibility and differential inclusion: Addressing honor-based violence in the Netherlands and Germany. *Social Politics: International Studies in Gender, State & Society, 27*(2), 187–211. https://doi.org/10.1093/sp/jxz004

Prevalence rates and crime characteristics **4**

Fuzzy data

Whether historically or presently, "honor" abuse, violence, and killings are reported worldwide and across a vast geographic territory. Estimates of "honor" crimes are based on unreliable data. In other words, fuzzy numbers (Viertl, 2011). As described in Chapter 3, without an agreed definition, it is not possible to collect reliable data to estimate the extent of the problem, locally, regionally, nationally, or globally. Therefore, regardless of the following three data sources, prevalence rates should be viewed cautiously:

- **Crime data.** When an incident of "honor" abuse, violence, or killing is formally reported, how this is recorded or classified varies within and across agencies, and from nation to nation. Therefore, any prevalence data collected by police departments or crime units are, at best, unreliable estimates (Cooney, 2019; Khan et al., 2015).
- **Victim services data.** Most victims are not aware of or in contact with general or specialist victim services (Khan, Saleem, & Lowe, 2018). If victims contact general services that do not provide specialist support for "honor" abuse and violence, they may decide not to disclose the full extent of their victimization (Lidman & Hong, 2018). Further, and in common with crime data, victim services data is unreliable due to differences in incident recording and classification (Khan, 2007; Ridley et al., 2023).
- **Research data.** Empirical investigations often use secondary data (e.g., crime data and/or victim services data). Alternatively, primary data can be collected for research studies (e.g., analysis of media articles and

DOI: 10.4324/9781003299950-6

social media posts). While these creative methods of data collection provide an insight into the nature of the problem, they do not provide a reliable estimate on the prevalence of "honor" abuse, violence, or killing.

Another obstacle to calculating the prevalence of "honor" abuse, violence, and killings is the significant issue of underreporting. As described in Chapter 5, victims face multiple and significant barriers to seeking help and support (see Box 4.1). These barriers are both internal and external. Internal barriers include the fears and beliefs victims themselves may have or knowledge they do not have (Begum et al., 2020). External barriers are formed due to other people's beliefs about "honor" abuse and violence, lack of specialist support, and race/ethnicity bias (Khan & Hall, 2020; Khan, 2021; Miles & Fox, 2023). Victims, particularly if they are visiting a different country or living overseas, may not know how to contact police or seek help from victim support agencies or may not feel safe doing so (Kazimirski et al., 2009; Magill, 2023). Services might be reluctant to support victims, believing "honor" abuse and violence are rooted in culture or religion and that intervening might be viewed as racist (Khan, 2007; Lidman & Hong, 2018). Therefore, in gauging the prevalence of "honor" abuse and violence, it is important to note victim reports made to the police and victim services are likely to be a vast underestimation (Khan et al., 2018).

Box 4.1 Barriers to formal reporting and help-seeking

Internal barriers	External barriers
• To protect their family's honor and reputation • To not act "dishonorable" by involving outsiders in a family matter • To protect abuser(s) or to preserve their relationship • To protect close family ties and unwillingness to get abuser(s) and/or family into trouble or shame them • To protect their religious identity and faith community as an impact of spiritual abuse • Fear of abuser(s) and/or family • Mistrust of or previous poor experience of police involvement • Unsure if the abuse is a crime • Unaware of victim support or specialist services	• Manipulation of professionals by abuser(s) and/or family • Physical presence or controlling behavior by abuser(s) and/or family • Myth of "perfect victim" and/or "typical perpetrator," and victim-blame attitudes • No access to interpreters • No access to refuge accommodation • Insecure immigration status • Racism or racial bias by police and/or service provider

While acknowledging the limitations of fuzzy data, the following sections summarize information from various sources to overview the prevalence of "honor" abuse, violence, and killings. The key characteristics of "honor" killing are also presented, specifically, the nature of the violence committed and the victim-perpetrator relationship. Victim-perpetrator dynamics are considered in detail in Chapters 5 and Chapter 6, respectively.

"Honor" killings—prevalence rates

"Honor" killings are the most extreme form of "honor" abuse and violence. Described as a global health problem, "honor" killings are reported in many parts of the world (Bhanbhro, Cronin de Chavez, & Lusambili, 2016, p. 198)— for instance, in Afghanistan, Albania, Australia, Bangladesh, Belgium, Brazil, Canada, Chechnya, Denmark, Ecuador, Egypt, Finland, France, Gaza Strip, Germany, India, Iran, Iraq, Israel, Italy, Jordan, Netherlands, Norway, Morocco, Pakistan, Russia, Saudi Arabia, Scotland, Sweden, Syria, Turkey, Uganda, the United Kingdom, the United States, and Yemen (Amnesty International, n.d.). An analysis of English-language media articles found 172 "honor" killings were recorded in 29 countries or territories between 1989 and 2009 (Chesler, 2010).

Although "honor" killings are reported in many geographic regions, in more recent times, they most commonly occur in the "patriarchy belt" (Caldwell, 1978). Also known as the "honor belt," these are a "band of countries stretching across the middle of the globe from north west Africa to south east Asia" (Cooney, 2019, p. 10). "Honor" killings are also reported among families from this diaspora internationally (Khan, 2018).

With regard to religion, "honor" killings are reported to occur in families of Christian, Sikh, Buddhist, and Hindu faiths (Cooney, 2019). "Honor" killings are frequently recorded in Muslim-majority countries, such as Iraq, Turkey, and Pakistan, prompting some authors (e.g., Chesler, 2010) to attribute these murders to the tenets of the Islamic religion. This myopic view is countered by other researchers who note "honor" killings are extremely rare in other Muslim-majority countries such as Indonesia, Malaysia, Nigeria, and Senegal (e.g., Bhanbhro et al., 2016; Teman, 2010). Also, as discussed in Chapters 1 to 3, there is good reason to be wary of explanations based solely on demographic factors, such as religion or culture. Further, fuzzy data can lead to fuzzy logic, leading people to make decisions based on imprecise information (Viertl, 2011). For instance, the classic correlation-causation fallacy, where a correlation (when variables are statistically associated) is confused with causality (when there is a cause-and-effect relationship).

As data on "honor" killings are not systematically collected by any government or crime agency, it is not possible to gauge the prevalence or key characteristics of these crimes. A commonly cited estimate is each year, over 5,000 women and girls are victims of "honor" killing in over 30 countries (United Nations Population Fund, 2000). Another potential problem is that some "honor" killings might be covered up or reframed (AlQahtani et al., 2022; Nur, 2021). The following estimations, therefore, represent only a proportion of "honor" killings, as "many cases are likely under-reported, camouflaged as suicides, accidents, disappearances or deaths from natural cause" (Cooney, 2014, p. 407).

Middle East

Yadav and Tripathi (2004) note that "honor" killings remain consistently high in Middle Eastern countries, specifically:

- In Jordan, 23 women (on average) were reported to be victims of "honor" killing each year. This figure represented around one-third of all murders nationally.
- In Lebanon, 38 "honor" killings were reported between 1996 to 1998; most victims were aged under 18 years.
- In Yemen, 400 women were reported to be victims of "honor" killing in 1997.
- In Egypt, there were 52 reports of "honor" killing.
- In the occupied Palestinian Territories, 27 "honor" killings were recorded in 2014, while there were 15 "honor" killings in 2015 (Gibbs et al., 2019). In a study with 535 women in this region, 41 (7.7%) reported there had been an "honor" killing in their family (Gibbs et al., 2019).
- In Iran, around 8,000 "honor" killings were recorded between 2010 and 2014 (Karami, Maleki, & Zahedi Mazandarani, 2019).

South Asia

- In Afghanistan, 243 "honor" killings were recorded between 2011 and 2013 (Afghanistan Independent Human Rights Commission, 2013).
- In a study with 1,461 women in Afghanistan, 33 (2.3%) reported there had been an "honor" killing in their family (Gibbs et al., 2019).

Although based on an estimate, Pakistan, which borders Afghanistan, is reported to have the highest number of "honor" killings:

- One-quarter of all cases worldwide are reported to occur in Pakistan alone, where "honor" killings of women constituted at least 21% of all homicides (male and female victims combined) (Nasrullah, Haqqi, & Cummings, 2009).

- A total of 1,957 "honor" killings were recorded between 2004 to 2007 (Nasrullah et al., 2009). Most victims were adults (82%), killed due to allegations of extramarital relationships (92%). In some cases, a woman was killed because she married a partner of her own choice (6%). At an average annual rate of 15 per million, most perpetrators were the victim's husband (38%), followed by their brother (22%). Community members were also reported to be involved, including local residents, neighbors, and employers (1.7%). The use of a firearm was reported in over half of cases (55%).
- Annual rates of "honor" killings rose from 869 (in 2013) to 1,000 (in 2014) and then 1,100 (in 2015) (Heydari, Teymoori, & Trappes, 2021).
- There were 4,388 "honor" killings recorded in Pakistan between 2010 to 2014. In 4,070 cases, victims were girls and women, and almost a quarter (22%; n = 926) were killed by brothers (Bhanbhro, 2021). The reasons they gave for committing sororicide included their sister having (or was alleged to have) a forbidden sexual relationship (50% of cases), or marrying without her family's consent, or to a man outside her social group (e.g., caste, clan, or tribe) (21% of cases). In the remaining cases, brothers claimed to have killed their sister to settle a dispute, or debt, or to take her share of family inheritance.
- In 2021, there were a total of 454 "honor" killings reported, 197 of which occurred in Sindh province (Human Rights Commission of Pakistan, 2022; Kamran, 2024).

In Pakistan, feudal culture and customs may be a significant predictor of "honor" killings, as the rates are highest in the Sindh province district, which is notorious for such crimes. A conservative estimate of "honor" killings in one region of Sindh is 55 to 60 a month, approximately two a day (Bhanbhro, 2021). In 2021, of the 454 reported cases of "honor" killings in Pakistan, 197 occurred in Sindh, with 226 victims, 82 of whom were men (Human Rights Commission of Pakistan, 2022). The following data was recorded on male victims, specifically (Human Rights Commission Pakistan, 2019; ACCORD, 2009):

- In 2007 (over 10 months), there were 104 reports of a male "honor" killing victim.
- In 2008, 96 out of 550 "honor" killing reports were of a male victim.
- In 2009 (over 3 months), 13 out of 53 "honor" killing reports were of a male victim.
- In 2014, 14 out of 837 "honor" killing reports were of a male victim.

Mediterranean and Northern Europe

Reports of "honor" killing vary across Mediterranean countries and northern Europe:

- In Turkey, around 53 women were victims of "honor" killing between 1994 and 1996 (Kogacioglu, 2004).
- In East Turkey, it was estimated between 25 to 75 "honor" killings are committed annually (Sev'er and Yurdakul, 2001), with 231 recorded in 2007 alone (Council of Europe Parliamentary Assembly, 2009) and 1,000 "honor" killings reported between 2003 and 2008 (US Department of State, 2009).
- In Turkey, a total of 188 "honor" killings were recorded between 2010 and 2015 (Nur, 2021). Most victims were aged under 36 years, living with a non-marital partner, and killed by their relatives with methods such as strangulation, hanging, electrocution, or poisoning.
- In an examination of 19 "honor" killings of men by men in Turkey between 2005 and 2008, Durbaş (2019) reported the following motivations accepted by the Turkish courts as mitigating circumstances:
  - Brothers of girls and women for harassing and/or raping them, or for having a relationship with the defendant's sister, or separating from the defendant's sister after starting a family.
  - Sons for having a relationship with the defendant's mother.
  - Male relatives (other than brothers, fathers, or husbands) for having a relationship with female relatives.
  - Other men in relation to adulterous relationships.

- In Italy, three "honor" killings of young women of Pakistani and Moroccan heritage were recorded within the last two decades. Hina Saleem, a 20-year-old, was murdered by her father and two of her brothers-in-law in 2006 (Kennedy, 2011). Saman Abbas, an 18-year-old, was murdered by her parents in 2021 (Ng, 2023). Sanaa Dafani, an 18-year-old girl, was murdered by her father in 2009 (Momigliano, 2010). Their deaths highlighted Italy's history of these "honor" crimes, which reportedly occurred in native Southern Italian populations until 1981 (De Cristofaro, 2018; Giuffrida, 2019).
- In Germany, the Federal Criminal Police (2011, cited in (Kizilhan, 2019) reported at least 55 "honor" killings (including attempted murders) between 1996 and 2005, with a total of 70 victims (48 female and 22 male). Of the victims killed, 36 were women, and 12 were men).

United Kingdom

As with other nations, the exact number of "honor" killings in the United Kingdom is not known, and prevalence rates are based entirely on estimates:

- While the police estimate around 12 murders annually were committed in the name of "honor," the media reported 29 "honor" killings or attempted killings between 2010 and 2014, indicating that the United Kingdom was the "honor" killing capital of Europe (Dyer, 2015).
- The Victim's Commissioner and Domestic Abuse Commissioner for England and Wales reported, in a joint letter to the UK Home Office report, that there were 75 new cases of "honor" killings in the United Kingdom between 2015 and 2020 (Jacobs & Baird, 2020).

North America

- The US Extremist Crime Database identified 16 known "honor" killings in the United States between 1990 and 2016 (Hayes, Mills, Freilich, & Chermak, 2018).
- In Canada, based on information gathered from criminal court cases and media reports, at least 12 "honor" killings appear to have been committed over a ten-year period (between 1999 and 2009) (Muhammad, 2010). This aligns with estimates of 10 to 15 "honor" killings that occurred in the first decade of the 21st century (Korteweg, 2012).

"Honor" killings—key characteristics

Three large-scale studies have examined the key characteristics of "honor" killings to determine the nature of the violence committed and victim-perpetrator relationships.

Chesler (2010) analyzed 230 cases reported in English-language media outlets in 29 countries or territories worldwide over two decades (1989 to 2009). Of all victims killed, 93% were women, with an average age of 23 years. Two types of "honor" killings, specific to female victims' age, were identified.

- First around 70% of victims were aged 25 years and under (average age, 17 years). They were most often killed by their families of origin (81% of the time).

- Second, around 30% of victims were aged 26 years or over (average age, 36 years). While these women were most often killed by their husbands, in almost half the cases (44%), their husbands were assisted by either their own families or by the victim's family.

Overall, two-thirds of all victims were killed by members of their family of origin, while almost half of these murders involved multiple perpetrators. Over half of these "honor" killings were described as torturous and involving severe suffering. This included being beaten, strangled, stoned, or burned to death; being stabbed multiple times; or being beheaded, raped, or gang raped before death. The use of torture and overkill, as a feature of "honor" killing, is discussed in Chapter 6, in the explanatory three-phase model of "honor" based abuse perpetration.

In the United States, Hayes, Freilich, and Chermak (2016) examined 40 "honor" killings committed between 1990 and 2014. Most frequently, the victim was the perpetrator's daughter (N = 9), his current wife (N = 5), niece (N = 4), or estranged wife (N = 3).

- *When the victim was a child of the perpetrator(s)*
  In 9 out of 16 of these cases (56%), a child was killed by a father or step-father. In terms of alleged motive, in five cases, the "honor" killing was blamed on the daughter's behavior. For instance, a father complained his daughter was becoming Westernized (N = 3), or his daughter resisted an arranged marriage (N = 1), or his daughter dated a non-Muslim (N = 1). Of the remaining four cases, the father stated that he murdered the child because of their mother's behavior.
- *When the perpetrator was a current or former intimate partner*
  Alleged motives for the "honor" killing included divorce/separation (N = 3), Westernized behavior or not following cultural ideals (N = 2), not preparing the preferred dinner (N = 1), or the perceived behavior of the victim's daughter (N = 2).
- *When a victim was an extended family member*
  There were six "honor" killings involving the death of at least one extended family member. In half of these cases, alleged motivations for the "honor" killing included the perpetrator's partner seeking a divorce or a daughter in the process of ending the relationship with the perpetrator. In the other half of these cases, it was reported family members were killed because the perpetrator interpreted either his intimate partner or his daughter's behavior as Westernized.

The alleged motives given by perpetrators for committing an "honor" killing are discussed elsewhere in this book. In Chapter 3, in relation to Problem 1: honor (and shame) as a justification. Also, in Chapter 6, in the explanatory three-phase model of "honor" abuse perpetration.

Also, in the United States, van Baak, Hayes, Freilich, and Chermak (2022) examined open-source data from the US Extremist Crime Database. They assessed 66 primary and corollary victims of 26 "honor" killings between 1990 and 2021.

- Most often, "honor" killing victims were daughters killed by their fathers, followed closely by intimate partners. In just over half of all cases, the perpetrator's partner was the primary victim.
- In total, 13 daughters were victims of an "honor" killing. Of note, in 54% of incidents, the daughter was targeted as a corollary victim, and the perpetrator's partner was the primary victim.

Van Baak et al. (2022, p. 22) concluded that "in the U.S., honor killings were most often committed because of a perceived misbehavior by the offender's current or former partner that violated the offender's honor—not necessarily because of the daughter's perceived misbehaviors."

These three investigations provide an insight into the extent and nature of so-called "honor" killings, which are the most extreme forms of "honor" abuse and violence. As "honor" crimes are vastly underreported, the number of non-fatal cases is thought to be far greater. Cases of "honor" abuse and violence might include episodic acts of physical (sometimes brutal) violence, but more commonly, they are nonphysical abuse—for instance, psychological abuse or coercive and controlling behavior.

"Honor" abuse and violence—prevalence

Various data sources were examined to provide estimates of nonfatal "honor" abuse and violence. As with cases of "honor" killings, these data represent only a fraction of cases due to unreliable incident recording, differences in classification, and underreporting (Khan, 2007). In the United Kingdom, one of the first nationwide estimates of "honor" abuse and violence was conducted by a national charity, the Iranian and Kurdish Women's Rights Organisation (*"Honour" attack numbers revealed by UK police forces*, 2011). Their analysis found in 2010, 2,823 cases of "honor" abuse and violence were reported to 39 police forces. Eight of these police forces recorded more than 100 cases each. Half a decade later, a national inspection of UK police forces found there were 251 referrals between 2014 and 2015 (Her Majesty's Inspectorate of Constabulary, 2015).

In the United Kingdom, from 2019 to date, the Home Office (2020, 2021, 2022, 2023) has reported mandatory data recorded by up to 43 police forces in England and Wales (see Table 4.1). This data shows police reports of "honor" abuse and violence are spread across the United Kingdom, and the types of offenses being recorded are diverse. Yet, data from other sources indicate these figures are not representative of the problem in the United Kingdom. For instance, there were

Table 4.1 Proportion of offenses involving so-called honor-based abuse mandatorily recorded by the police since 2019, by offense category, in England and Wales

	2019–2020	2020–2021	2021–2022	2022n2023
Total offenses	**2,024**	**2,725**	**2,887**	**2,905**
Incidents noted but not recorded as crime[a]	—	—	1,871	
Offense breakdown	HBA[b] = 1,810 FGM[c] = 74 FM[d] = 140	HBA = 2,522 FGM = 78 FM = 125	HBA =2,669 FGM = 77 FM = 141	HBA = 2,649 FGM = 84 FM= 172
Offense category	%	%	%	%
Controlling and coercive behavior	—	14	17	19
Assault without injury	28	16	14	12
Assault with injury	17	15	14	16
Threats to kill	10	8	9	9
Kidnapping	10	6	6	8
Malicious communications	7	7	8	6
Rape of a female aged 16 and over	6	6	6	6
Harassment	5	5	5	4
Stalking	2	5	6	6
Cruelty to children/ young persons	2	2	2	2
Public fear, alarm, or distress	1	1	1	1
All other offenses	10	14	11	10

a First data on the number of "honor" abuse–related incidents that have not resulted in the recording of a notifiable crime (e.g., police may have been alerted to a possible offense, but there was not sufficient information to warrant the recording of a crime)
b HBA: "Honor"-based abuse
c FGM: Female genital mutilation
d FM: Forced marriage

12,107 calls logged by a national charity with a telephone helpline specifically for "honor" based abuse and forced marriage, and of these, 70% were related to victim support (Khan, Khan, Adisa, Kumari, & Allen, 2021). This point is illustrated further when police data on forced marriage alone is compared with data from the Forced Marriage Unit (2023), a national advice or support center, as shown in Table 4.2.

Table 4.2 Forced Marriage Unit statistics (2012 to 2023)

Year	Cases	Age (if known)	Gender	Focus countries (country to which forced marriage risk relates)	UK distribution	Disabilities	LGBT
2012	**1,485**	13% 15 or under 22% 16–17 years 30% 18–21 years 19% 22–25 years 8% 26–30 years 8% 31+ years	82% female 18% male	60	England – 71% NI – 0.2% Scotland – 1% Wales – 1% Unknown – 27%	114	22
2013	**1,302**	15% 15 or under 25% 16–17 years 33% 18–21 years 15% 22–25 years 8% 26–30 years 7% 31+ years	82% female 18% male	74	England – 75.8% NI – 0.3% Scotland – 2.9% Wales – 1.6% Unknown – 19.4%	97	12
2014	**1,267**	11% 15 or under 11% 16–17 years 17% 18–21 years 14% 22–25 years 7% 26–30 years 3% 31+ years	79% female 21% male	88	England – 54.1% NI = 0.7% Scotland – 2.3% Wales – 1.4% Unknown – 20%	135	8
2015	**1,220**	14% 15 or under 13% 16–17 years 20% 18–21 years 15% 22–25 years 9% 26–30 years 8% 31+ years	80% female 20% male	67	England – 79% NI – <5 cases, % not given Scotland – 2% Wales 2% Unknown – 18%	141	29

(Continued)

Table 4.2 (Continued)

Year	Cases	Age (if known)	Gender	Focus countries (country to which forced marriage risk relates)	UK distribution	Disabilities	LGBT
2016	**1,428**	15% 15 or under 11% 16–17 years 20% 18–21 years 15% 22–25 years 10% 26–30 years 8% 31+ years	80% female 20% male	69	England – 81% NI – 0 Scotland – 2% Wales – 1% Unknown – 16%	140 (10%)	30 (2%)
2017	**1,196**	16% 15 or under 14% 16–17 years 18% 18–21 years 12% 22–25 years 10% 26–30 years 12% 31+ years	77.8% female 21.4% male	65	England – 89.8% NI – <5 cases, % not given. Scotland – 1.5% Wales – 1.4% Unknown – 7%	125 cases (12.1%)	21 (1.8%)
2018	**1,507**	19% 15 or under 16% 16–17 years 19% 18–21 years 14% 22–25 years 9% 26–30 years 10% 31+ years	75% female 18% male	64	England – 81% NI – <5 cases, % not given. Scotland – 2% Wales – 2% Unknown – 17%	93 cases (6%)	12 cases (1%)
2019	**1,355**	15% 15 or under 12% 16-17 years 22% 18-21 years 14% 22-25 years 10% 26-30 years 11% 31+ years	80% female 19% male	66	England – 80% NI – <5 cases, % not given Scotland – 2% Wales – 3% Unknown – 16%	137 cases (10%)	29 cases (2%)

Year	Total	Age	Gender		Country		
2020	759(C19)	15% 15 or under 11% 16–17 years 22% 18–21 years 15% 22–25 years 11% 26–30 years 16% 31+ years	79% female 21% male	54	England – 80% NI – <5 cases, % not given Scotland – 2% Wales – 2% Unknown – 17%	66 cases (9%)	19 cases (3%)
2021	337(C19 and change in recording practice)	22% 15 or under 13% 16–17 years 18% 18–21 years 17% 22–25 years 9% 26–30 years 17% 31+ years	74% female 26% male	32	England – 81% NI – <5 cases, % not given. Scotland – 2% Wales – 2% Unknown – 13%	53 cases (16%)	6 cases (2%)
2022	302	14% 15 or under 47% 16–17 years 26% 18–21 years 13% 22–25 years 15% 26–30 years 12% 31+ years	78% female 22% male	25	England – 91% NI – x Scotland – x Wales 2% Unknown – 7%	62 cases (19%)	5 cases
2023	283	12% 15 or under 13% 16–17 years 18% 18–21 years 16% 22–25 years 15% 26–30 years 25% 31+ years	69% female 31% male	30	England – 91% NI – x Scotland – 2% Wales – x Unknown – 7%	67 cases (24%)	2 cases

Source: Forced Marriage Unit, 2023.

End of chapter reflections

This chapter pieced together fragmented estimates of "honor" abuse, violence, and killings provided by numerous sources, including crime data, victim services data, and research data. This overview indicates the scale of the problem is far greater than this fuzzy data suggests. Even without reliable data, this overview establishes "honor" abuse and violence as a problem faced by many children, young people, and adults in many parts of the world at risk of many types of harm committed by different people motivated by any number of reasons, yet all committed in the name of so-called "honor".

References

ACCORD- Austrian Centre for Country of Origin and Asylum Research and Documentation. (2009, July 9). *Pakistan: Honour killing of men; availability of state protection.* https://www.refworld.org/docid/4a5604292.html

Afghanistan Independent Human Rights Commission. (2013, August 26). *National Inquiry on Rape and Honor Killing in Afghanistan Report.* https://www.refworld.org/pdfid/5a1fe8144.pdf

AlQahtani, S. M., Almutairi, D. S., BinAqeel, E. A., Almutairi, R. A., Al-Qahtani, R. D., & Menezes, R. G. (2022). Honor killings in the Eastern Mediterranean region: A narrative review. *Healthcare, 11*(1), 74. https://doi.org/10.3390/healthcare11010074

Amnesty International. (n.d.). *The horror of "honour killings," even in US.* https://www.amnestyusa.org/the-horror-of-honor-killings-even-in-us/

Begum, R., Khan, R., Brewer, G., & Hall, B. (2020). "They will keep seeing young women murdered by men. Enough is enough-we have seen too many women lose their lives". lessons for professionals working with victims of 'honour' abuse and violence. *Genealogy, 4*(3), 1–12. https://doi.org/10.3390/genealogy4030069

Bhanbhro, S. (2021). Brothers Who Kill: Murders of Sisters for the Sake of Family Honour in Pakistan. In A. Buchanan, & A. Rotkirch (Ed.) *Brothers and Sisters* (pp. 297–312). Palgrave Macmillan. https://doi.org/10.1007/978-3-030-55985-4_17

Bhanbhro, S., Cronin De Chavez, A., & Lusambili, A. (2016). Honour based violence as a global public health problem: a critical review of literature. *International Journal of Human Rights in Healthcare, 9*(3), 198–215. https://doi.org/10.1108/IJHRH-10-2015-0032

Caldwell, J. C. (1978). A theory of fertility: From high plateau to destabilization. *Population and Development Review,* 553–577. https://www.jstor.org/stable/1971727

Chesler, P. (2010). Worldwide trends in honour killings. *Middle East Quarterly, 17*(2), 3–11 https://www.meforum.org/2646/worldwide-trends-in-honor-killings

Cooney, M. (2019). *Execution by family: A theory of honor violence.* Routledge.

Cooney, M. (2014). Death by family: Honor violence as punishment. *Punishment & Society, 16*(4), 406–427. https://doi.org/10.1177/1462474514539537

Council of Europe Parliamentary Assembly. (2009, June 8). *The urgent need to combat so-called 'honor crimes'.* http://assembly.coe.int/nw/xml/XRef/Xref-XML2HTML-en.asp?fileid=12696&lang=EN

De Cristofaro, E. (2018). The crime of honor: an Italian story. *Historia et ius, 14,* 1–12. http://www.historiaetius.eu/uploads/5/9/4/8/5948821/14_15_de_cristofaro.pdf

Durbaş, B. (2019). The so-called honour killings of men by men in Turkey. In Idriss, M. M. (Ed.). *Men, Masculinities, and Honour-Based Abuse* (pp. 150–166). Routledge.

Dyer, E. (2015). *'Honour' killings in the UK*. Henry Jackson Society. https://henryjackson society.org/wp-content/uploads/2015/01/Honour-Killings-in-the-UK.pdf

Forced Marriage Unit. (2023, June 20). *Forced Marriage Unit statistics*. https://www.gov.uk/government/collections/forced-marriage-unit-statistics

Gibbs, A., Said, N., Corboz, J., & Jewkes, R. (2019). Factors associated with 'honour killing' in Afghanistan and the occupied Palestinian territories: Two cross-sectional studies. *PLoS One*, 14(8), e0219125. https://doi.org/10.1371/journal.pone.0219125

Giuffrida, A. (2019, March 10). Italy accused of restoring honour killing defence after lenient femicide rulings. *The Guardian*. https://www.theguardian.com/world/2019/mar/18/italy-jail-terms-reduced-men-killed-wives-femicide

Hayes, B. E., Mills, C. E., Freilich, J. D., & Chermak, S. M. (2018). Are honor killings unique? A comparison of honor killings, domestic violence homicides, and hate homicides by far-right extremists. *Homicide Studies*, 22(1), 70–93. https://doi.org/10.1177/1088767917736796

Hayes, B. E., Freilich, J. D., & Chermak, S. M. (2016). An exploratory study of honor crimes in the United States. *Journal of Family Violence*, 31, 303–314. https://doi.org/10.1007/s10896-016-9801-7

Her Majesty's Inspectorate of Constabulary (HMIC). (2015, December). *The depths of dishonour: Hidden voices and shameful crimes - An inspection of the police response to honour-based violence, forced marriage and female genital mutilation*. https://assets-hmicfrs.justiceinspectorates.gov.uk/uploads/the-depths-of-dishonour.pdf

Heydari, A., Teymoori, A., & Trappes, R. (2021). Honor killing as a dark side of modernity: prevalence, common discourses, and a critical view. *Social Science Information*, 60(1), 86–106. https://doi.org/10.1177/0539018421994777

Home Office. (2023, October 19). *Statistics on so called 'honour-based' abuse offences, England and Wales, 2022 to 2023*. https://www.gov.uk/government/statistics/so-called-honour-based-abuse-offences-2022-to-2023/statistics-on-so-called-honour-based-abuse-offences-england-and-wales-2022-to-2023

Home Office. (2022, October 20). *Statistics on so called 'honour-based' abuse offences, England and Wales, 2021 to 2022*. https://www.gov.uk/government/statistics/statistics-on-so-called-honour-based-abuse-offences-england-and-wales-2021-to-2022/statistics-on-so-called-honour-based-abuse-offences-england-and-wales-2021-to-2022

Home Office. (2021, December 9). *Statistics on so called 'honour-based' abuse offences, England and Wales, 2020 to 2021*. https://www.gov.uk/government/statistics/statistics-on-so-called-honour-based-abuse-offences-england-and-wales-2020-to-2021/statistics-on-so-called-honour-based-abuse-offences-england-and-wales-2020-to-2021

Home Office. (2020, December 16). *Statistics on so called 'honour-based' abuse offences recorded by the police*. https://www.gov.uk/government/statistics/statistics-on-so-called-honour-based-abuse-offences-england-and-wales-2019-to-2020/statistics-on-so-called-honour-based-abuse-offences-recorded-by-the-police

'Honour' attack numbers revealed by UK police forces. (2011, December 3). BBC News. https://www.bbc.co.uk/news/uk-16014368

Human Rights Commission of Pakistan. (2022). *State of Human Rights in 2021*. https://hrcp-web.org/hrcpweb/wp-content/uploads/2020/09/2022-State-of-human-rights-in-2021.pdf

Human Rights Commission Pakistan. (2019). *Stats: Honour crimes men/women*. http://hrcp-web.org/hrcpweb/campaigns/

Iranian and Kurdish Women's Rights Organisation. (2011, December 3). *Nearly 3000 cases of 'honour' violence every year in the UK*. https://ikwro.org.uk/2011/12/03/nearly-3000-cases-of-honour-violence-every-year-in-the-uk/

Jacobs, N. & Baird, V. (2020, December 18). *Joint letter to the Home Secretary on honour-based abuse*. https://victimscommissioner.org.uk/document/letter-to-home-office-on-honour-based-abuse/

Kamran, A. (2024). Addressing honour killings: a smart policy design and implementation approach to Karo-Kari in Rural Sindh. *The Public Sphere: Journal of Public Policy, 12*(1), 70–85. https://psj.lse.ac.uk/articles/159

Karami, G., Maleki, A., & Zahedi Mazandarani, M. J. (2019). Sociological explanation of the phenomenon of honor killings (for the sake of honor) in Khuzestan Province during 2011–2015. *Quarterly Journal of Social Development, 13*(3), 81–116. http://10.22055/qjsd.2019.14563

Kazmirski, A., Keogh, P., Kumari, V., Maisie, R., Gowland, S., Purdon, S. & Khanum, N. (2009). *Forced Marriage: Prevalence and Service Response*. Department of Children, Schools & Families, London. http://oro.open.ac.uk/44739/

Kizilhan, J. I. (2019). The impact of culture and belief in so-called honour killings a comparative study between honour murders and other perpetrators of violence in Germany. *Journal of Forensic Investigation, 7*(1), 1–7. https://www.dhbw-vs.de/files/content/03_FORSCHUNG/TCultHS/Publikationen/Papers/2019-09-03-Honour-killings-JFI-2330-0396-07-0043.pdf

Kennedy. D. (2011, February 10). Murdered by her father for becoming a Western woman. *BBC News*. https://www.bbc.co.uk/news/world-europe-12416394

Khan, Y., Khan, R., Adisa, O., Kumari, M., & Allen, K., (2021). *'Honour' abuse, violence, and forced marriage in the UK. Police cases (incidents and charges) and specialised training: 2018 and 2019*. Honour Abuse Research Matrix (HARM), University of Central Lancashire, UK. https://clok.uclan.ac.uk/36438/1/%27Honour%27%20abuse%20violence%20and%20forced%20marriage%20in%20the%20UK%20%282021%29.pdf

Khan, R. (2021). *Domestic abuse policy guidance for UK universities*. Honour Abuse Research Matrix (HARM), University of Central Lancashire, UK. https://clok.uclan.ac.uk/37526/7/37526%20Domestic%20Abuse%20Policy%20Guidance%20for%20UK%20Universities%202021.pdf

Khan, R. & Hall, B. (2020). *Harmful traditional practices in the workplace: guidance for best practice*. Honour Abuse Research Matrix (HARM), University of Central Lancashire, UK. https://clok.uclan.ac.uk/32803/7/32803%20Harmful%20Traditional%20Practices%20in%20the%20Workplace%20-%20Guidance%20for%20Best%20Practice%202020.pdf

Khan, R., Saleem, S., & Lowe, M. (2018). "Honour"-based violence in a British South Asian community. *Safer Communities, 17*(1), 11–21. https://doi.org/10.1108/SC-02-2017-0007

Khan, R. (2018). Attitudes towards "honor" violence and killings in collectivist cultures: Gender differences in Middle Eastern, North African, South Asian (MENASA) and Turkish populations. In J. L. Ireland, P. Birch, & C. A. Ireland (Eds.), *International Handbook in Aggression: Current Issues and Perspectives* (pp. 216–226): Routledge. https://doi.org/10.4324/9781315618777

Khan, R., Willan, V. J., Lowe, M., Robinson, P., Brooks, M., Irving, M., … & Bryce, J. (2015). Assessing victim risk in cases of violent crime. *Safer Communities, 14*(4), 203–211. https://doi.org/10.1108/SC-05-2015-0020

Khan, R. (2007). Honour-Related Violence (HRV) in Scotland: A cross-and multi-agency intervention involvement survey. *International Journal of Criminology*, 1–8. https://clok.uclan.ac.uk/13518/

Kogacioglu, D. (2004). The tradition effect: Framing honor crimes in Turkey. *Differences: A Journal of Feminist Cultural Studies, 15*(2), 119–151. https://muse.jhu.edu/article/170546

Korteweg, A. C. (2012). Understanding honour killing and honour-related violence in the immigration context: Implications for the legal profession and beyond. *Canadian Criminal Law Review, 16*(2), 135–160. http://cdhpi.ca/sites/cdhpi.ca/files/korteweg_cclr-under standing-honour-killing.pdf

Lidman, S., & Hong, T. (2018). "Collective violence" and honour in Finland: A survey for professionals. *Journal of Aggression, Conflict and Peace Research, 10*(4), 261–271. https://doi.org/10.1108/JACPR-09-2017-0319

Magill, S. (2023). The "epidemic within the pandemic": meeting the needs of racially minoritised women experiencing domestic abuse during the Covid-19 pandemic. *Journal of Aggression, Conflict and Peace Research, 15*(3), 187–200.https://doi.org/10.1108/JACPR-05-2022-0717

Miles, C., & Fox, C. (2023). Collaboration, risk and 'just' outcomes: challenges and opportunities in policing HBA. *Policing and Society, 33*(5), 501–517. https://doi.org/10.1080/1043 9463.2022.2147174

Momigliano. A. (2010, February 2). Honor killing by any other name. *The Nation.* https://www.thenation.com/article/archive/honor-killing-any-other-name/

Muhammad, A. A. (2010). *Preliminary examination of so-called 'honour' killings in Canada.* Presented to Family, Children and Youth Section, Department of Justice, Canada. https://canada.justice.gc.ca/eng/rp-pr/cj-jp/fv-vf/hk-ch/hk_eng.pdf

Nasrullah, M., Haqqi, S., & Cummings, K. J. (2009). The epidemiological patterns of honour killing of women in Pakistan. *European Journal of Public Health, 19*(2), 193–197. https://doi.org/10.1093/eurpub/ckp021

Ng, K. (2023, December 20). Italian court jails parents for life over 'honour killing' of Pakistani teen. *BBC News.* https://www.bbc.co.uk/news/world-europe-67769159

Nur, N. (2021). An assessment of intimate partner femicide in the name of honour in Turkey: a retrospective epidemiological study. *Psychiatria Danubina, 33*(2), 152–157. https://doi.org/10.24869/psyd.2021.152

Ridley, K., Almond, L., Bafouni, N., & Qassim, A. (2023). 'Honour'-based abuse: A descriptive study of survivor, perpetrator, and abuse characteristics. *Journal of Investigative Psychology and Offender Profiling, 20*(1), 19–32. https://doi.org/10.1002/jip.1602

S'er, A. (2005). In the name of fathers: honour killings and some examples from South-eastern Turkey. *Atlantis: Critical Studies in Gender, Culture & Social Justice, 30*(1), 129–145. https://journals.msvu.ca/index.php/atlantis/article/view/866/859

Sev'er, A. & Yurdakul, G. (2001). Culture of honor, culture of change: A feminist analysis of honor killings in rural Turkey. *Violence against Women, 7*(9), 964–998. https://doi.org/10.1177/10778010122182866

Terman, R. (2010). To specify or single out: should we use the term "honor killing"?. *Muslim World Journal of Human Rights, 7*(1), 1–39. https://doi.org/10.2202/1554-4419.1162

United Nations Population Fund. (2000, January 1). *The state of the world population 2000. Lives together, worlds apart: men and women in a time of change.* New York. http://www.unfpa.org/swp/2000/english

US Department of State. (2009, February 25). *County reports on human rights practices.* https://2009-2017.state.gov/j/drl/rls/hrrpt/2008/eur/119109.htm

van Baak, C., Hayes, B. E., Freilich, J. D., & Chermak, S. M. (2022). Honor killings in the United States from 1990 to 2021: Primary victims and corollary victims. *Crime & Delinquency,* 1–30. https://doi.org/10.1177/00111287221128482

Viertl, R. (2011). *Statistical methods for fuzzy data.* John Wiley & Sons.

Yadav, S. & Tripathi, A. (2004). For the sake of honour: But whose honour? 'Honour crimes' against women. *Asia-Pacific Journal on Human Rights and the Law 5*(2): 63–78. https://heinonline.org/HOL/LandingPage?handle=hein.journals/apjur5&div=15&id=&page=

Victims

5

Who are the victims, and why are they victimized?

Gender inequality, a key feature of "honor" abuse, violence, and killings, is not unique to collectivist honor cultures, specific countries, or any one religion. An analysis of 75 countries, representing 80% of the global population, found nine out of ten men and women were biased toward women, almost one-third of whom believed it acceptable for a husband to beat his wife (United Nations Development Programme, 2020). "Honor" abuse and violence, as with family violence and child abuse more generally, occurs on a spectrum with severity and injury ranging from mild to extreme (R. Khan, 2018). The distinct difference is one or more family members are perpetrators, and the motive for controlling or harming the victim is to protect or defend their family's so-called "honor," a belief that may be endorsed and enforced by any number of community members.

Regardless of individual traits, personal circumstances, or social status, victims of "honor" abuse and violence suffer myriad detrimental effects that can be acute and chronic. Coercive and controlling behaviors, such as harassment, stalking, and malicious communication, are prominent features in "honor" abuse victimization (see Table 4.1, Chapter 4). Although physical violence is less common than coercive control, when used, it can be excessive. For instance, a notable feature of "honor" killings is overkill, as described in Chapter 6. Whether violence is used or not, the harm extends beyond physical injury and contributes to psychological trauma resulting from internalized shame and public shaming (Khan, Saleem, & Lowe, 2018; Mafura & Charura, 2022).

DOI: 10.4324/9781003299950-7

Many of these unique features are evidence in the tragic and highly publicized so-called "honor" killing of 17-year-old Shafilea Ahmed in England in 2004. Her mother and father were later sentenced to life imprisonment for her murder. Eight family members were arrested on conspiracy to pervert the course of justice—proceedings against them were dropped (Dyer, 2015). It was reported that Shafilea's parents subjected her to significant physical violence and emotional abuse throughout her childhood and that she was severely deprived of food and water. Shafilea went missing while receiving treatment for extensive damage to her throat after she drank bleach—reportedly a suicide attempt after she resisted a forced marriage in Pakistan, which her parents claimed had shamed them. Shafilea's poems were of interest to the police during their investigations, as they described her emotional state and helplessness while living at home. For instance, her poem "Happy Families" (Onal, 2012, p. 6):

> I don't pretend like we're the perfect family no more
> Desire to live is burning
> My stomach is turning
> But all they think about is honour
> I was a normal teenage kid
> Didn't ask 2 much
> I just wanted to fit in
> But my culture was different
> But my family ignored
> Now I'm sitting here
> Playing happy families
> Still crying tears

Five months after she went missing, Shafilea's dismembered and decomposed remains were found by the police, deliberately hidden 70 miles (110 km) from her home (Dyer, 2015).

Chapter 3 details that in collectivist honor cultures, children are socialized to follow rigid gender codes. Each person ("me") is expected to maintain the honorable status of their family and community ("we") by complying with gender codes. Although each family and its members will observe these codes to different degrees, in the main, there is a clear distinction between female and male honor codes. Females are expected to behave in a way that is passive, agreeable, virtuous, and submissive. Males are expected to be hypermasculine and act tough, assertive, dominant, and strong-willed (Khan, 2018; Vandello, 2016). It is also important that each person follows these gendered honor codes in a way that can be observed by others—both inside and outside their home.

As illustrated in Figure 5.1, girls and women maintain their own and their family's honorable status by guarding their own virginity and fidelity. For instance, girls must not have sex until marriage. Married women must remain faithful to their husbands. The same expectation does not apply to males. As illustrated in Figure 5.2, boys and men maintain their own and their family's honor using hypermasculine behavior to guard their female relative's chastity, using coercion and punishment to control them if they deem it necessary. Males also oversee honor codes in other males in their family and community to ensure fathers, sons, uncles, nephews, and in-laws are each maintaining their male honor. In this way, "honor" abuse, violence, and killings are consequences of extreme conformity to honor codes. Specifically, where family and community members collectively and strictly monitor, curb, and punish each other's behavior to ensure that rigid gender codes are followed in the belief of so-called honor. The different roles that perpetrators take in maintaining these strict honor codes and their motivation for doing so are detailed in the three-phase model of "honor" abuse perpetration in Chapter 6.

While the impact of "honor" abuse and violence might be similar for different victims, the reason why victims are targeted differs according to a number of characteristics.

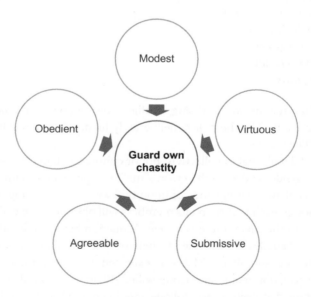

Figure 5.1 Female honor codes emphasize guarding her own chastity (obeying male authority)

Figure 5.2 Male honor codes emphasize the use of hypermasculinity to guard the chastity of female relatives

Female victims

It is clear from all available data that victims are typically women and girls. This is clearly illustrated in the prevalence data on "honor" abuse, violence, and killings in Chapter 4. Much of what is known about victims of "honor" abuse, violence, and killings is drawn from studies on South Asian, Middle Eastern, and North African females—in their countries of birth or in diasporic communities worldwide (Lowe, Khan, Thanzami, Barzy, & Karmaliani, 2018). Far less acknowledged are victims with other racial, ethnic, and cultural identities, including women and girls of Mediterranean, Turkish, or Roma heritage or in Gypsy Traveler communities (Asquith, 2015; Caffaro, Ferraris, & Schmidt, 2014; De Cristofaro, 2018; Giuffrida, 2019). Also overlooked is female victimization reported in Catholic, Jewish, Hindu, and Sikh families and communities (Bhanbhro, de Chavez, & Lusambili, 2016; Chesler & Bloom, 2012; Pall & Kaur, 2021).

Chapter 3 details how dual identities based on race/ethnicity stereotypes are used to create the myth of "perfect" victims and "typical" perpetrators. One consequence of this myth is that victims and perpetrators who do not fit these stereotypes may be overlooked. Academics and victim support organizations have challenged these myths. For instance, Unchained at Last (2024), a survivor-led organization in the United States campaigning to end forced and child marriage, estimate around 300,000 children from various faiths and religions with multiple racial, ethnic, identities were married in the United States between 2000 and 2018. Specifically, 86% were girls aged under 18 (some as young as 10 years) who were married to adult men aged over 18 years. Further, since 2000, around 60,000 marriages "occurred at an age or with a spousal age difference that should have constituted a sex crime under the relevant state's law" (Reiss, 2021, s.9).

Male victims

While victims of "honor" abuse, violence, and killings are overwhelmingly female, there is an increasing awareness of male victimization (Bhanbhro, 2023; Idriss, 2020, 2022). Males are often targeted for "honor" abuse and violence due to their relationships with females accused of behaving "dishonorably" (Begum, Khan, Brewer, & Hall, 2020; Steinke, 2013). As discussed in the following section, boys and men may be targeted if they are homosexual or if they do not conform to gendered expectations of behaving in an overtly masculine way (Khan & Lowe, 2020; Lowe et al., 2021).

Table 4.2 in Chapter 4 shows between 2012 to 2023, males consistently represented around one-fifth of cases reported to the United Kingdom's Forced Marriage Unit (2023). In an analysis of "honor" killings, Chesler (2010) estimated around 7% of victims worldwide were male:

> The murdered male victims were usually perceived as men who were unacceptable due to lower class or caste status, because the marriage had not been arranged by the woman's family of origin, because they were not the woman's first cousin, or because the men allegedly engaged in pre- or extramarital sex. Men were rarely killed when they were alone; 81 percent were killed when the couple in question was together.

In India, 1,000 men from 10 cities or towns reported a high lifetime experience of "honor"-based violence (99.7%: 45.1% often and 41.7% sometimes). Exposure to "honor" abuse and violence was strongly associated with a range of sociodemographic factors, including age, income, religion, education, and region (Broom et al., 2012).

Although there are no official data in the United Kingdom, male victims of "honor" killings are reported in the British media. Dyer (2015) notes,

[O]ne man was killed alongside his wife and daughter by his ex-wife's family. Another male victim was the partner of a British Pakistani woman, both of whom were attacked by the woman's ex-husband. ... While both survived, the man is now paralysed. In another case...a man and his wife were shot because they refused to marry their daughters to the perpetrator's nephews.

(p. 16)

Also that a teenager was "stabbed to death by the father and teenage brothers of his girlfriend. ... During the trial, the court heard that this murder took place due to the 'shame and dishonour'" brought on the family as a result of the relationship (Dyer, 2015, p. 16). In another case, 19-year-old Arash Gorbani was killed in 2004 by the father and teenage brothers of his girlfriend, Manna Begum. During the trial, the court heard the perpetrators stabbed Arash 46 times because Manna had refused an arranged marriage due to her relationship and pregnancy with Arash and that their relationship had brought "shame and dishonour" to the family (*"Honour killing" son set for prison release*, 2021).

Lesbian, gay, bisexual, and transgender (LGBT) victims

Cases of "honor" abuse, violence, and killings are reported in LGBT communities. Research studies have explored the experiences of victims who are white European (Donovan, Magić, & West, 2023; Rogers, 2017) and British South Asian (e.g., Khan, Hall, & Lowe, 2017; Lowe et al., 2021). Forced marriage is a concern, as illustrated in Table 4.2 in Chapter 4, which shows between 2012 to 2022, LGBT victims represented a proportion of cases reported to the United Kingdom's Forced Marriage Unit (2023). Given the reluctance of victims to disclose abuse to protect family honor and to avoid "shame," these figures are likely to be an underestimation (Khan et al., 2017; Khan & Lowe, 2020).

Much of the "honor" abuse inflicted on LGBT people stems from attempts to control their sexuality and/or gender identity, which reflects the antigay, homophobic, or transphobic abuse, violence, and murders reported in many countries where LGBT sexualities are denounced (Asquith, 2015; Mendos et al., 2020; Rogers, 2017; Khan et al., 2017). One extreme is the reported state-sponsored, so-called gay genocide in Chechnya after the leader condoned the "honor" killing of gay people (Gerbaka, Richa, & Tomb, 2021).

Other vulnerability factors

Other factors linked with "honor" abuse, violence, and killings include physical disability or mental health issues (Aplin, 2018). Table 4.2 in Chapter 4 shows between 2012 to 2022, victims with disabilities represented a notable proportion of cases reported to the United Kingdom's Forced Marriage Unit (2023). A UK study found men and women with learning disabilities were equally at risk of being a victim of forced marriage, unlike the general population, where women are far more likely to be victims (Clawson & Fyson, 2017). In these cases, families often forced daughters and sons into marriage to obtain a permanent carer, partly due to a cultural misunderstanding of the nature of disabilities. The study's authors state,

> [I]n the United Kingdom forced marriage may…be associated with particular minority ethnic groups, but it is…important not to assume that forced marriage only occurs in specific and readily-identifiable communities. Notably, one of the first reported cases in England of a person with a learning disability being forced to marry was of a white British woman being sold into marriage by her brother.
>
> (p. 812)

Rooted in religious conservativism, apostates who identify as being nonreligious within a religious household may be victimized for dishonoring and shaming the collective beliefs of their family and community. A study of 154 respondents who had left their religious faith (Christian, Muslim, Hindu, and Jewish) reported they had been a victim of assault. However, only nine officially reported their abuse to the police. The study's authors state, "Given some families' concerns about honor, one would expect people labeled as apostates or non-religious (e.g., atheist, humanist, secular, or nontheist) to be at risk of discrimination, maltreatment, and abuse within religiously inclined households" (Parekh & Egan, 2021, p. 11685).

What types of harm are victims subjected to?

As detailed in Chapter 2, unlike other forms of family violence, child abuse, and domestic homicide, "honor" abuse is often perpetrated by more than one relative, may include people known to the family, and can occur over a long period of time (Alam, Khan, & Graham-Kevan, 2023; Ridley, Almond, Bafouni, & Qassim, 2023). The key characteristics of the harm committed, and perpetrator-victim relationships are outlined in Chapter 4.

Four types of "honor" abuse and violence

In Sweden, four themes underlying "honor" based abuse were identified in a study with 11 female victims (16 to 20 years) with non-Swedish parents (Björktomta, 2019). As shown in Box 5.1, these themes were symbolic, social, psychological, and physical violence. These themes, which included a range of subtle and hard psychological and physical abuse perpetrated from childhood, are reported across multiple other studies (e.g., Aplin, 2017, 2019; Bates, 2018). At the root of the abuse, and against the backdrop of parental/paternal dominance, men and boys policed their female relatives, with a focus on chastity, to ensure their behavior was deemed "honorable" and respectful. Of note, physical

---

Box 5.1 Four types of "honor" based abuse (Björktomta, 2019)

1. **Symbolic violence**: Girls were socialized to behave in line with social and gender norms—to be obedient and learn that chastity was a symbol of family honor. Parents conveyed to daughters how they were permitted (and not permitted) to behave using nonverbal messages, body language, and emotions.
2. **Social violence**: These were daily honor-based expectations in the girl's daily life that, when crystalized, restricted her everyday actions. The conflict between parental authority and the daughter's needs led to tension, a defining feature of the parent-child relationship.
3. **Psychological violence**: A merger of symbolic and social violence ensured that family norms were followed to preserve family honor. Examples included silence, isolation, verbal abuse, degradation, humiliation, confinement, abandonment, rejection, and threats (of violence and death). More common in families with physically violent fathers, mothers used emotional blackmail to force daughters to obey their fathers via hostile attitudes and conduct (e.g., silence). This provoked shame and guilt, which forced obedience and restricted daughters' ability to act.
4. **Physical violence**: Mostly to punish girls when they are disobedient or do not follow family/gender norms. Punishment was inflicted by male relatives (fathers and brothers) for violating family norms and damaging family honor and reputation. When inflicted by mothers, it was mainly related to children's upbringing, family conflict, or family separation (due to migration).

violence was not always needed to maintain control, as violence was expressed in other, nonverbal ways, such as "a rigorous eye" (Björktomta, 2019, p. 458).

Coercive control—"murder by language"

Coercive and controlling behavior is a common feature of family violence, child abuse, and domestic homicide; it is implicit in "honor" abuse, violence, and killings. Coercive control involves an array of deliberate and persistent acts (or tactics) used to control and manipulate someone by regulating and monitoring their behavior. Control is achieved by threats, intimidation, restrictions, deprivation, and isolation (Stark, 2023). Typically, the victim's words, behavior, and actions are closely monitored and scrutinized by a perpetrator to ensure their demands are followed, under the threat of punishment for digressing from this expectation (Stark, 2023).

In England and Wales, *controlling or coercive behavior* is an offense that includes people in an intimate personal relationship (whether they live together or not), those who live together and have either been in an intimate relationship, or members of the same family (Home Office, 2024). In Chapter 4, Table 4.1 shows that of the "honor" abuse and violence offenses recorded by the police in England and Wales, between 14% and 17% were for controlling or coercive behavior, representing one of the largest proportion of offenses (Home Office, 2021, 2022, 2023).

Coercive control is powerful and dehumanizing because it interweaves psychological, physical, sexual, emotional, financial, and / or other abuse, enabling a perpetrator to weaken and entrap a victim in a life monitored and controlled by them (McMahon & McGorrery, 2020). The impact of coercive and controlling behavior in "honor" abuse, violence, and killings may be particularly powerful. Specifically, as noted in Chapter 3, any number of family members—close or distant, in person or online, over a long period of time—might be involved in monitoring the victim's behavior (Janssen, Sanberg, & van der Sluis, 2011).

A salient feature of coercive and controlling behavior in "honor" abuse, violence, and killings is community gossip. In extreme cases, community gossip has been termed "murder by language" (Chesler, 2015) or "death by family" (Cooney, 2014). Gossip, a basic human tendency, transcends all historical, cultural, and geographical boundaries (Levin & Arluke, 1985). Research studies show people are motivated to gossip for a number of positive reasons. For instance, bonding with group members, exchanging information, venting emotions, and maintaining social order (Bechtoldt, Beersma, & Dijkstra, 2020). Less positive functions of gossiping include a desire to be aggressive and to advance personal interest at the cost of others. In patriarchal "honor" cultures, gossip can be used to control and dominate females by scandalizing and shaming them, particularly daughters and wives. Awwad (2001) states,

> Gossip is at the center of a family's code of honor. Once shame threatens the family's honor, it becomes a concern of the entire community and not just the family. Therefore, the family is pressured through the continuation of gossip to take the necessary steps to purify or "purge" its honor. This results in restoring the family's social standing in the neighborhood and the community. ... Gossip is a tool used by community members to spread the unpleasant reality or truth that a certain family's honor has been tarnished, and therefore a family's social and prestigious status is in danger. Gossip then becomes a tool used to remind the family of its shame.
>
> (p. 45)

In this way, community gossip can be viewed as collective coercive control, the impact of which can be powerful. Collective coercive control is reported to have an accumulative and eroding impact on victims, who are under constant surveillance, inside or outside of their homes by any number of relatives, peers, neighbors, community members, locally or in other regions, in person or online (Gengler, Alkazemi, & Alsharekh, 2021; Janssen et al., 2011).

Studies have explored how "honor" abuse and violence function as a form of culturally driven coercive control. A study in New Zealand, with 27 high school girls mostly of Indian heritage, found coercive control was a prominent feature in their dating relationships. They also witnessed coercive control in the relationships of women and girls they knew (Mayeda, Cho, & Vijaykumar, 2019). Shown in Box 5.2, these adolescents reported coercive controlling behavior occurred at three levels: (1) family/microlevel, (2) community/mesolevel, and (3) macrolevel. These themes are reported in other studies with girls born and/or raised in the West who try to meet others' expectations across two conflicting spheres: at home (where intimate relationships were not discussed and dating was forbidden) and in their social lives (where dating and sexual activity were rife and the norm). Feeling alienated in both spheres, girls in this predicament struggle to meet family obligations and social expectations while sacrificing their own wants (Begum et al., 2020; Bhattacharyya, 2009; Gigi Durham, 2004). Further, a fear of their parents and community learning they dated often meant these girls were unlikely to seek help when ending an abusive relationship. In the main, they remained in abusive relationships to avoid shaming their families and/or risking being excluded from the local community (Couture-Carron, 2020; Sandhu & Barrett, 2020, 2024; Tongsing, 2016). Help-seeking from non-family members of external services can also bring dishonor (Huisman, 1996; Tongsing & Barn, 2017).

Box 5.2 Three levels of culturally driven coercive control (Mayeda, Cho, & Vijaykumar, 2019)

1 Family/microlevel

- Monitoring (real-life and digital) whereabouts, dress, friendships, and interactions.
- When girls attempt to end their relationships, boyfriends (described as "insanely jealous" or "weirdly possessive") threaten to involve a girl's parents.
- Coercive control (via threats, intimidation, and restrictions) was used to exploit honor codes and blackmail girls who feared their parents would learn they were in a relationship.

2 Community/mesolevel

- There were few opportunities to discuss relationships or to disclose abuse due to "honor" codes and gender expectations of girls and women in the wider community, limiting contact with external agencies.
- Girls talked about being policed by a powerful force of "community gossip" and "unofficial media." Abusive males relied on community codes of shame to ensure she was compliant to prevent her from leaving the relationship.

3 Macrolevel

- The importance of "reputation" was pressed at the expense of women's physical and mental health.
- Migrant women were subjected to coercive and controlling behavior by manipulation under a real/false threat that their visa would be revoked if they challenged abusive partners.

What is the psychosocial impact on victims?

The psychological and social impact of "honor" abuse and violence on victims can be profound. Research studies into multiple perpetrator domestic abuse—a key feature of "honor" abuse and violence—report this is linked with poor mental and physical health, domestic homicide, homelessness among women, and severe mental illness and suicidality (Salter, 2014). Studies show an oppressive home life characterized by parental monitoring, controlling, and scrutiny—common in "honor" abuse and violence—can lead to a sense of entrapment and dehumanization (Khan, 2018; Sandhu & Barrett, 2024). Dehumanization affects people's cognitions and emotions. By limiting a person's agency and autonomy, the very core of that person can be undermined and affect their identity and status in two main ways (Bastian & Haslam, 2011). First, when someone's equal status is not recognized, this is associated with feelings of guilt and shame. Second, when someone's basic existence is not recognized, this is related to feelings of sadness and anger. Even with attempts to resist dehumanization, being subjected to dehumanizing abuse and violence can change the way a victim views themselves, others, and the world.

When aspects of dehumanization are internalized, this can lead to self-dehumanization (Way & Rogers, 2017). The association was found in a study of female victims of intimate partner violence in Iran (Shahbazi, Sadeghi, & Panaghi, 2023). These victims reported feeling powerless and inferior in their marriage, aggravated by negative social attitudes toward women. This led to a sense of self-dehumanization, which invoked negative cognitions, emotions, and coping strategies. It is unsurprising that growing up in an oppressive environment leads to the development of coping strategies. A US study with South Asian Muslim female victims of "honor" abuse and violence noted that from childhood, they heard stories of women who had no options to escape abusive husbands, in-laws, or other relatives (Ayyub, 2000). Consequently, they reported a lack of autonomy, as they were raised to be submissive, obedient, and compliant, and to take care of their families' needs over their own. Ultimately, parents expected young women to tolerate and totally submit to the authority of their husbands and their families, encouraging them to accept this as their fate.

For women and girls living in oppressive environments, submissive traits were tactics for survival that came with adverse consequences for their mental and physical health (Begum et al., 2020; Khan et al., 2018). The following section overviews what is known about victims' detrimental coping behaviors and survival strategies while living at home and when they have run away from home.

Coping strategies when living at home

Self-harm and suicide

Victims of "honor" abuse and violence frequently report feelings of guilt, shame, sadness, and anger—traits associated with dehumanization—which, in turn, are linked with mental ill-health, including self-harm and suicide. A study with over 200 young people in the northwest of England found "honor" abuse and violence victims did not report their experiences to anyone and hid their injuries to protect their family's honor (Khan et al., 2018). Over half of these victims reported feelings of anger at the perpetrator(s), while a quarter reported feeling scared of their abuser(s). However, due to being isolated from others, they could not confide in anyone about their victimization, which impacted their mental health. Over two-thirds of these young people reported feelings of anxiety, nearly three-quarters felt depressed, a third had self-harmed as a direct result of their abuse, and a similar number ran away from home to escape their abuse. Over 10% attempted suicide.

Studies have linked compliance with rigid honor codes with trauma in women, leading to self-harm. In a study of South Asian British women, self-mutilation stemmed from the trauma of living in a "cultural limbo" of balancing their dual identity inside and outside their home, burdened by cultural expectations, without personal autonomy, and as a form of penance to punish themselves for transgressions (Mafura & Charura, 2022). A study participant stated,

> I was kept at home to cook, clean, and look after the family. I was being groomed to be a wife and this broke me…it was horrific…the tears, the stress and what happened to me. … I still had to do it because that's what we do…and I did.
>
> (p. 464)

Another woman stated,

> My worst phase was probably three years ago when I ended up having over 50 stitches in my arms over a period of a week. I was so scared of myself; I never would have envisaged myself doing so much damage to my own body.
>
> (p. 465)

Self-harm is one of the most common reasons for medical admission in the United Kingdom (Özen-Dursun, Kaptan, Giles, Husain, & Panagioti, 2023). In the United States, there are an estimated 200,000 suicide attempt-related hospitalizations each year (Canner, Giuliano, Selvarajah, Hammond, & Schneider, 2018). As ethnicity is not recorded on death certificates in the United Kingdom, it is not possible to assess links between ethnicity and suicide rates. Nonetheless, studies show British South Asian women report cultural conflicts with family are strongly associated with suicide ideation (Hicks & Bhugra, 2003; Husain, Waheed, & Husain, 2006), and they are considered to be an "at-risk" group for self-harm (Bhui, McKenzie, & Rasul, 2007), suicide attempts (Forte et al., 2018), and suicide (McKenzie, Bhui, Nanchahal, & Blizard, 2008). For instance, hospital emergency admissions data over four years showed British South Asian women (aged 16 to 24 years) were at 1.5 greater risk for self-harm than white women

(Husain et al., 2006). The main psychosocial stressors linked with self-harm included conflicts between and within family members, especially disagreements over family values, personal choices in relationships, and family pressuring arranged marriages (Hicks & Bhugra, 2003).

High rates of suicide in women of South Asian heritage are reported across the world and are seen as a major global health crisis (Bhanbhro, de Chavez, & Lusambili, 2016; Patel & Gaw, 1996). One of the starkest reports is that across the world, nearly 40% of all suicides are reported to occur in India (Patel & Gaw, 1996; Patel et al., 2012; Patel et al., 2021) and that Indian women account for over a third of all global suicides in the 15–39 age group (Garcia et al., 2022), with suicides related to "family issues" or "marriage-related issues." Post-COVID-19 studies show that housewives represent the greatest increase in suicides in India, with 61 suicides each day and over half of the total number of women who killed themselves (Garcia et al., 2022). Their suicides were linked to oppressive marital homes and relentless domestic abuse.

Garcia et al. (2022) estimated around half of these women's suicides were dowry-related (i.e., payment, such as money or property paid by the bride's family to the groom or his family at the time of marriage), and thus are reported as accidental deaths due to getting burned or falling. As noted in Chapter 4, in an assessment of "honor" killing worldwide, Cooney (2014, pp. 407) considered "many cases are likely under-reported, camouflaged as suicides, accidents, disappearances or deaths from natural cause."

A study in rural Bangladesh concluded that when women are victims of rape, there are regarded as "spoiled," and their reputation cannot be restored. Numerous women were beaten, murdered, or driven to suicide because of the "dishonor" that rape or illegitimate pregnancy brought upon the family (Fauveau, Wojtyniak, Koenig, Chakraborty, & Chowdhury, 1989). Gorar (2022) highlighted that given the vulnerability of "honor" abuse victims, "honor" suicides and forced suicides are likely to be unreported and unrecognized by legal systems.

"Honor" suicides were defined as

> [w]here "honor" killings are robustly prosecuted, families may deploy a strategy of forcing women to kill themselves in order to remain technically innocent of murder. This is particularly associated with regions of Turkey; however, it may not be clear in any country whether an individual woman has committed suicide due to direct coercion, to spare her brother the jail sentence he might face as her murderer, whether an outright murder has been disguised as self-killing, or whether a woman has killed herself due to the unbearable pressures of the restrictions upon her life and her family's disfavour or abuse.

(p. 310)

Forced suicide was defined as

> [a]t the extreme end of honour suicide, and could be considered as murder. It is a form of honour killing where a female member of society violates the alleged honour codes of that society by bringing shame to her family. In order to be technically innocent of murder, families force the victim to commit suicide. The victim is locked in a room with a weapon (knife, gun or rope) and ordered by family or relatives to take her own life. The door is not opened until she has killed herself. Like honour killings, forced suicides are the choice of a family and imposed on a victim by the family. Forced suicides are likely to be presented as honour suicides (committed voluntarily by the victim) or as "accidental" deaths carried out by the perpetrators to escape criminal liability.
>
> (p. 311)

In a frank statement about the predicament of female "honor" abuse and violence victims, Begum et al. (2020, p. 3) contend, "These women are at high risk of attempting to erase themselves, while being at risk of being erased by others."

Coping strategies: run away from home

When victims cannot disclose or seek support for "honor" abuse and violence at home, they may decide to run away (Chaudhuri, Morash, & Yingling, 2014). Running away from home is a coping strategy reported by many British South Asian women attempting to avoid forced marriages (Britton et al., 2002; Khan et al., 2018; Shalev Greene & Alys, 2016; Sharp, 2010, 2015). An examination of nonreported and police-reported cases of missing people found young British South Asian women were more likely to go missing following conflict with parents about marriage when compared with women of other ethnic origins (Biehal Mitchell, & Wade, 2003). Sharp (2013) highlights the clear overlap between the profiles of young people aged under 18 years old who go missing and forced marriage victims, and the role that loss of honor and shame plays in this:

> Because they are fearful of the loss of honour and respect, for themselves and their families as a result of running away, these young people may be more likely than those from other ethnic groups to continue coping with a difficult home situation and only leave as a last resort.
>
> (pp. 97–98)

Victims report significant challenges in attempts to leave home, as their movements may be restricted under the surveillance of family and community members (Begum et al., 2020). In the United Kingdom, government and police guidelines recognize both female and male victims of forced marriage may regard running away from home as their only option (Home Office Communications Directorate, 2000; Newiss, 2005; Sharp, 2015). Victims, regardless of their racial and ethnic identity, may be forced to flee with their children.

Khan (2017), a refugee worker in the United Kingdom, reported,

> Over the years, we have provided refuge for many families fleeing forced marriage and "honour"-based abuse. These families often face added barriers to rebuilding their lives after overcoming abuse and homelessness. Some families may always have to manage the threat of violence from family and extended community members (beyond the individuals they "know"), which can cause extreme and life-lasting fear and isolation. For example, a South Asian woman fleeing forced marriage may always need to manage these risks by avoiding things like ethnic food shops and local mosques; parts of the local community that could have embraced and provided protection to her and her children. We recently supported an Eastern European woman and her 8 year old daughter. Anna (the mother) had suffered domestic abuse from her partner for 6 years. When he threatened to take their daughter to Iraq for an arranged marriage, Anna called the police, and a joint decision was made that Anna and her daughter must leave the area. After years of abuse, far from her family and with little command of English, Anna and her daughter faced homelessness.

Homelessness and sexual exploitation risk

When someone runs away from home to escape abuse, they will encounter multiple, potentially hazardous, unknowns. One of these is the imminent threat of homelessness. When "honor" abuse victims with minoritized racial and ethnic identities run away from home, they face the additional fear of encountering prejudice based on their race, religion, or faith (Magill, 2023). Victims with insecure immigration status and no recourse to public funding are caught in limbo—without a home or access to support services (Proudman, & Lloyd, 2023).

Studies report the extreme lengths some families go to find victims who have run away or fled a forced marriage. In a UK study with British South Asian female and male victims (aged 15 to 18), methods included falsely accusing them of theft; utilising extended family networks; contacting community leaders; paying "bounty hunters" and private investigators; tracing individuals through medical and dental records, national insurance numbers, benefit records or school/college records; circulating details of the missing person to local taxi drivers, members of the community and shopkeepers; and contacting people within the Asian community who hold positions of power, such as social services and Members of Parliament.

(Sharp, 2015, pp. 99–100)

Two women in this study had run away from home to escape a forced marriage but had nowhere to go. Each identified a man they had met on social media as someone to offer help, yet in both cases, the men detected their vulnerability and then exploited them, which put them at risk for sexual exploitation.

Family estrangement

Studies have identified estrangement as a long-term consequence of escaping "honor" abuse. Whether ostracized (excluded) or scapegoated (publicly blamed), the impact of estrangement can be devastating and is identified as a form of dehumanization (Bastian & Haslam, 2011). Chhina (2017) explained the act of running away publicly challenges and opposes cultural norms. Therefore, when a victim runs away, their dissent is swiftly labeled as "shameful" and "dishonorable," leading them to be ostracized from their family and community.

This response can be viewed as the risk of "social death"—that is, families also report being at risk of social ostracism, exclusion, stigma, and rejection if they do not shun and/or punish the victim for transgressing "honor" codes. In a study of "honor" killings in Palestine, Khatib, Edge, and Speed (2020) noted,

Family members perceived themselves not only as mourners but also as victims. They had lost their loved one in a violent death and society was stigmatizing and treating them as "deviants or outcasts."... Respondents reported that they had to be seen publicly as agreeing with the crime to appear united. This led to further judgment by the community and further ostracism.

(p. 1018)

A UK study with 15 South Asian women (aged 23 to 57 years) reported their experience of leaving a violent relationship where they had chosen their partner, with and without their family's support (Sandhu & Barrett, 2020). A third of these women still suffered family estrangement resulting from choosing their own partner.

One participant disclosed that her family estrangement was exploited by her abusive partner, which further worsened her sense of isolation:

> "Your family didn't care about you. They didn't support you." Basically, I had to put up with whatever was thrown at me. ... It was my choice, I did this. I chose to be with him and now I'm in this situation. I have to put up with it. I have to try and make it work.
>
> (p. 10)

An authoritarian parenting style, common in families who strictly observe honor codes, places emphasis on strict obedience, discipline, and control, as well as being in line with honor codes (Bhattacharyya, 2009). Studies in Bangladesh show that children raised in this way tend to exhibit anxious and withdrawn behaviors, lack self-reliance, and rely on authority figures to make decisions, diminishing their sense of personal value and responsibility (Arafat, Akter, Islam, Shah, & Kabir, 2020). These traits are elements of dehumanization noted earlier in this chapter. These adults are often submissive and conform easily. Authoritarian parenting often leads to familial interdependence throughout the lifespan. Consequently, adult children are socialized to remain emotionally dependent on, and loyal to, their parents (Munaf, 2015). Studies show that the high levels of family interdependence common in collectivistic honor cultures are associated with far greater negative responses to family ostracism (Yaakobi, 2021). As a result, parents can exert significant amounts of influence in all aspects of life, whether they live close to each other or not, and elders are respected and revered as wise authority figures, regardless of how they behave toward their children. It is significant that the threat and fear of being socially ostracized are reported to be motivations for perpetrating "honor"-based crimes and play a part in pressuring someone to commit an "honor" killing (Doğan, 2014, 2016, 2018; Rahman, 2021).

End of chapter reflections

This chapter highlights the need for researchers and professionals in criminal justice systems and public protection to recognize "honor" abuse, violence, and killings as a distinct form of family violence, child abuse, and domestic homicide. To understand these victims' unique experiences, researchers and practitioners must be aware of why victims are targeted for abuse, the different types of harm they are subjected to, and the strategies victims use to cope with and survive in the face of everyday oppression and suffering. The significance of this is noted by Begum et al. (2020), who state "honor" abuse victims and survivors

> often suffer three-fold: the harm inflicted by their abusers, self-blame born out of being shamed and the poor response from mainstream support services. An additional layer of suffering occurs when they also experience racism or are overlooked by external organisations due to cultural ignorance or fear of being racist.

(p. 4)

References

Alam, A., Khan, R., Graham-Kevan, N. (2023). Family "honor" killings. In T. K. Shackelford (Ed.), *Encyclopedia of Domestic Violence* (pp.1–4). Springer. https://doi.org/10.1007/978-3-030-85493-5528-1

Aplin, R. (2019). *Policing UK honour-based abuse crime*. New York: Springer International Publishing.

Aplin, R. L. (2018). Honour based abuse: The response by professionals to vulnerable adult investigations. *Journal of Aggression, Conflict and Peace Research, 10*(4), 239–250. https://doi.org/10.1108/JACPR-09-2017-0320

Aplin, R. (2017). Exploring the role of mothers in 'honour' based abuse perpetration and the impact on the policing response. *Wome's Studies International Forum, 60*, 1–10. https://doi.org/10.1016/j.wsif.2016.10.007

Arafat, S. Y., Akter, H., Islam, A., Shah, M. M. A., & Kabir, R. (2020). Parenting: Types, effects and cultural variation. *Asian Journal of Pediatric Research, 3*(3), 32–36. https://doi.org/10.9734/AJPR/2020/v3i330130

Asquith, N. (2015). Honour, violence, and heteronormativity. *International Journal for Crime, Justice and Social Democracy, 4*(3), 73–84. https://search.informit.org/doi/10.3316/informit.252495412146320

Awwad, A. M. (2001). Gossip, scandal, shame and honor killing: A case for social constructionism and hegemonic discourse. *Social Thought & Research, 24*(1/2), 39–52. https://www.jstor.org/stable/23250074

Ayyub R. (2000). Domestic violence in the South Asian Muslim immigrant population in the United States. *Journal of Social Distress and the Homeless, 9*(3), 237–248. https://doi.org/10.1023/A:1009412119016

Bastian, B., & Haslam, N. (2011). Experiencing dehumanization: Cognitive and emotional effects of everyday dehumanization. *Basic and Applied Social Psychology, 33*(4), 295–303. https://doi.org/10.1080/01973533.2011.614132

Bates, L. (2018). Females perpetrating honour-based abuse: Controllers, collaborators or coerced?. *Journal of Aggression, Conflict and Peace Research, 10*(4), 293–303. https://doi.org/10.1108/JACPR-01-2018-0341

Bechtoldt, M. N., Beersma, B., & Dijkstra, M. T. (2020). Why people gossip and what it brings about: Motives for, and consequences of, informal evaluative information exchange. *Frontiers in Psychology, 11*, 24. https://doi.org/10.3389/fpsyg.2020.00024

Begum, R., Khan, R., Brewer, G., & Hall, B. (2020). "They will keep seeing young women murdered by men. Enough is enough-we have seen too many women lose their lives". lessons for professionals working with victims of 'honour' abuse and violence. *Genealogy,* 4(3), 1–12. https://doi.org/10.3390/genealogy4030069

Bhattacharyya, S. (2009). Intergenerational conflicts in Indian American Adolescents. *International Journal of Diversity in Organizations, Communities, and Nations,* 9(4), 171–182. https://doi.org/10.18848/1447-9532/CGP/v09i04/39752

Bhanbhro, S. (2023). Honour Crimes. In P. Ali, & M. M. Rogers (Eds.), *Gender-Based Violence: A Comprehensive Guide* (pp. 285–297). Springer. https://doi.org/10.1007/978-3-031-05640-6

Bhanbhro, S., de Chavez, A. C., & Lusambili, A. (2016). Honour based violence as a global public health problem: a critical review of literature. *International Journal of Human Rights in Healthcare,* 9 (3), 198–215. https://doi.org/10.1108/IJHRH-10-2015-0032

Bhui, K., McKenzie, K. & Rasul, F. (2007). Rates, risk factors & methods of self-harm among minority ethnic groups in the UK: a systematic review. *BMC Public Health* 7, 336. https://doi.org/10.1186/1471-2458-7-336

Biehal, N., Mitchell, F. and Wade, J. (2003) *Lost from view: Missing persons in the UK.* Bristol: The Policy Press.

Björktomta, S. B. (2019). Honor-based violence in Sweden–Norms of honor and chastity. *Journal of Family Violence,* 34(5), 449–460. https://doi.org/10.1007/s10896-019-00039-1

Britton, L., Chatrik, B., Coles, B., Craig, G., Hylton, C., & Mumtaz, S. (2002). *Missing ConneXions: The Career Dynamics and Welfare Needs of Black and Minority Ethnic Young People at the Margins.* International Specialist Book Services (distributor for Policy Press), 920 NE 58th Ave., Suite 300, Portland, OR 97213–3786. https://eric.ed.gov/?id=ED474777

Broom, A., Sibbritt, D., Nayar, K. R., Nilan, P., & Doron, A. (2012). Me's experiences of family, domestic and honour-related violence in Gujarat and Uttar Pradesh, India. *Asian Social Science,* 8(6), 3–10. http://doi.org/10.5539/ass.v8n6p3

Caffaro, F., Ferraris, F., & Schmidt, S. (2014). Gender differences in the perception of honour killing in individualist versus collectivistic cultures: Comparison between Italy and Turkey. *Sex Roles,* 71(9), 296–318. https://doi.org/10.1007/s11199-014-0413-5

Canner, J. K., Giuliano, K., Selvarajah, S., Hammond, E. R., & Schneider, E. B. (2018). Emergency department visits for attempted suicide and self harm in the USA: 2006–2013. *Epidemiology and Psychiatric Sciences,* 27(1), 94–102. https://doi.org/10.1017/S2045796016000871

Chaudhuri, S., Morash, M., & Yingling, J. (2014). Marriage migration, patriarchal bargains, and wife abuse: A study of South Asian women. *Violence against Women,* 20(2), 141–161. https://doi.org/10.1177%2F1077801214521326

Chesler, P. (2015). When women commit honor killings. *Middle East Quarterly,* 22(4). https://www.meforum.org/5477/when-women-commit-honor-killings?source=post_page

Chesler, P. & Bloom, N. (2012). Hindu vs Muslim honor killings, *Middle East Quarterly,* 19(3), 43–52. https://www.meforum.org/3287/hindu-muslim-honor-killings

Chesler, P. (2010). Worldwide trends in honour killings. *Middle East Quarterly,* 17(2), 3–11. https://www.meforum.org/2646/worldwide-trends-in-honor-killings

Chhina, R. (2017). *An exploration of the experiences of challenging Izzat among six South Asian women City.* University of London. http://yorksj.idm.oclc.org/login?url=https://search.ebscohost.com/login.aspx?direct=true&db=edsble&AN=edsble.738450&site=eds-live&scope=site

Clawson, R., & Fyson, R. (2017). Forced marriage of people with learning disabilities: A human rights issue. *Disability & Society,* 32(6), 810–830. https://doi.org/10.1080/09687599.2017.1320271

Cooney, M. (2014). Death by family: Honor violence as punishment. *Punishment & Society, 16*(4), 406–427. https://doi.org/10.1177/1462474514539537

Couture-Carron, A. (2020). Shame, family honor, and dating abuse: Lessons from an exploratory study of South Asian Muslims. *Violence Against Women, 26*(15–16), 2004–2023. https://doi.org/10.1177/1077801219895115

De Cristofaro, E. (2018). The crime of honor: An Italian story. *Historia et ius, 14,* 1–12. http://www.historiaetius.eu/uploads/5/9/4/8/5948821/14_15_de_cristofaro.pdf

Doğan, R. (2018). Do women really kill for honor? Conceptualizing women's involvement in honor killings. *Deviant Behavior, 39*(10), 1247–1266. https://doi.org/10.1080/01639625.2017.1420454

Doğan, R. (2016). The dynamics of honor killings and the perpetrators' experiences. *Homicide studies, 20*(1), 53–57. https://doi.org/10.1177/1088767914563389

Doğan, R. (2014). The profiles of victims, perpetrators, and unfounded beliefs in honor killings in Turkey. *Homicide studies, 18*(4), 389–416. https://doi.org/10.1177/1088767914538637

Donovan, C., Magić, J., & West, S. (2023). Family abuse targeting queer family members: An argument to address problems of visibility in local services and civic life. *Journal of Family Violence,* 1–13. https://doi.org/10.1007/s10896-023-00651-2

Dyer, E. (2015). 'Honour' killings in the UK. Henry Jackson Society. https://henryjacksonsociety.org/wp-content/uploads/2015/01/Honour-Killings-in-the-UK.pdf

Fauveau, V., Wojtyniak, B., Koenig, M. A., Chakraborty, J., & Chowdhury, A. I. (1989). Epidemiology and cause of deaths among women in rural Bangladesh. *International Journal of Epidemiology, 18*(1), 139–145. https://doi.org/10.1093/ije/18.1.139

Forced Marriage Unit. (2023, June 20). *Forced Marriage Unit statistics.* https://www.gov.uk/government/collections/forced-marriage-unit-statistics

Forte, A., Trobia, F., Gualtieri, F., Lamis, D. A., Cardamone, G., Giallonardo, V., … & Pompili, M. (2018). Suicide risk among immigrants and ethnic minorities: a literature overview. *International Journal of Environmental Research and Public Health, 15*(7), 1438. https://doi.org/10.3390/ijerph15071438

Garcia, E. C., Vieira, P. S. C., de Andrade Viana, R. C., Mariano, F. C., de Brito, M. I. B., Neto, J. D. A. F., … & Neto, M. L. R. (2022). Domestic violence and suicide in India. *Child Abuse & Neglect, 127,* 105573. https://doi.org/10.1016/j.chiabu.2022.105573

Gengler, J. J., Alkazemi, M. F., & Alsharekh, A. (2021). Who supports honor-based violence in the Middle East? Findings from a national survey of Kuwait. *Journal of Interpersonal Violence, 36*(11–12), NP6013–NP6039. https://doi.org/10.1177/0886260518812067

Gerbaka, B., Richa, S., & Tomb, R. (2021). Honor Killings and Crimes; Familial and Tribal Homicide. In B. Gerbaka, S. Richa, & R. Tomb (Eds.), *Child Sexual Abuse, Exploitation and Trafficking in the Arab Region* (pp. 183–228). Springer International Publishing. https://doi.org/10.1007/978-3-030-66507-4

Gigi Durham, M. (2004). Constructing the "new ethnicities": media, sexuality, and diaspora identity in the lives of South Asian immigrant girls. *Critical Studies in Media Communication, 21*(2), 140–161. https://doi.org/10.1080/07393180410001688047

Gorar, M. (2022). Honour Suicide and Forced Suicide in the UK. *The Journal of Criminal Law, 86*(5), 308–326. https://doi.org/10.1177/00220183221115294

Giuffrida, A. (2019, March 10). Italy accused of restoring honour killing defence after lenient femicide rulings. *The Guardian.* https://www.theguardian.com/world/2019/mar/18/italy-jail-terms-reduced-men-killed-wives-femicide

Hicks, M. H. R., & Bhugra, D. (2003). Perceived causes of suicide attempts by UK South Asian women. *American Journal of Orthopsychiatry, 73*(4), 455–462. https://doi.org/10.1037/0002-9432.73.4.455

Home Office. (2024, January 3). *Policy paper. Amendment to the controlling or coercive behavior offence.* https://www.gov.uk/government/publications/domestic-abuse-bill-2020-factsheets/amendment-to-the-controlling-or-coercive-behaviour-offence

Home Office. (2023, October 19). *Statistics on so called 'honour-based' abuse offences, England and Wales, 2022 to 2023.* https://www.gov.uk/government/statistics/so-called-honour-based-abuse-offences-2022-to-2023/statistics-on-so-called-honour-based-abuse-offences-england-and-wales-2022-to-2023

Home Office. (2022, October 20). *Statistics on so called 'honour-based' abuse offences, England and Wales, 2021 to 2022.* https://www.gov.uk/government/statistics/statistics-on-so-called-honour-based-abuse-offences-england-and-wales-2021-to-2022/statistics-on-so-called-honour-based-abuse-offences-england-and-wales-2021-to-2022

Home Office. (2021, December 9). *Statistics on so called 'honour-based' abuse offences, England and Wales, 2020 to 2021.* https://www.gov.uk/government/statistics/statistics-on-so-called-honour-based-abuse-offences-england-and-wales-2020-to-2021/statistics-on-so-called-honour-based-abuse-offences-england-and-wales-2020-to-2021

'Honour killing' son set for prison release. (2021, May 4). BBC News. https://www.bbc.co.uk/news/uk-england-oxfordshire-56988067

Huisman K. A. (1996). Wife battering in Asian American communities. Identifying the service needs of an overlooked segment of the U.S. population. *Violence Against Women, 2*(3), 260–283. https://doi.org/10.1177/1077801296002003003

Husain, M. I., Waheed, W., & Husain, N. (2006). Self-harm in British South Asian women: psychosocial correlates and strategies for prevention. *Annals of General Psychiatry, 5*(1), 1–7. https://doi.org/10.1186/1744-859X-5-7

Home Office Communications Directorate. (2000). *A Choice by Right: The Report of the Working Group on Forced Marriage.* https://edm.parliament.uk/early-day-motion/17745/a-choice-by-right-the-report-by-the-working-group-on-forced-marriages

Idriss, M. M. (2022). Abused by the patriarchy: Male victims, masculinity, "honor"-based abuse and forced marriages. *Journal of Interpersonal Violence, 37*(13–14), NP11905–NP11932. https://doi.org/10.1177/0886260521997928

Idriss, M. M. (Ed.). (2020). *Men, masculinities, and honour-based abuse.* Routledge.

Khan, R., & Lowe, M. (2020). Homophobic 'honour' abuse experienced by South Asian gay men in England. In M. M. Idriss (Ed.), *Men, masculinities, and honour-based abuse* (pp. 95–113). Routledge. https://doi.org/10.4324/9780429277726

Khan, R., Hall, B., & Lowe, M. (2017). *"Honour" abuse: The experience of South Asians who identify as LGBT in North West England. (Summary report prepared for Lancashire Constabulary).* Honour Abuse Research Matrix (HARM). http://clok.uclan.ac.uk/20996/7/20996%20LGBT%20Honour%20Report%20-%20Final%20%282018%29.pdf

Khan, S. (2017, September 18). *Reflections of a refuge worker: Forced marriage, 'honour'-based abuse and homelessness.* SafeLives. Ending Domestic Abuse. Spotlight #5: Homelessness and Domestic abuse. https://safelives.org.uk/practice_blog/reflections-refuge-worker-forced-marriage-%E2%80%98honour%E2%80%99-based-abuse-and-homelessness

Khan, R. (2018). Attitudes towards "honor" violence and killings in collectivist cultures: Gender differences in Middle Eastern, North African, South Asian (MENASA) and Turkish populations. In J. L. Ireland, P. Birch, & C. A. Ireland (Eds.), *International Handbook in Aggression: Current Issues and Perspectives* (pp. 216–226). Routledge. https://doi.org/10.4324/9781315618777

Khan, R., Saleem, S., & Lowe, M. (2018). "Honour"-based violence in a British South Asian community. *Safer Communities, 17*(1), 11–21. https://doi.org/10.1108/SC-02-2017-0007

Khatib, S., Edge, D., & Speed, S. (2020). On the road to social death: a grounded theory study of the emotional and social effects of honor killing on families—A Palestinian perspective. *Violence Against Women, 26*(9), 1008–1032. https://doi.org/10.1177/1077801219847289

Janssen, J., Sanberg, R., & van der Sluis, D. (2011). Virtual honour: violating and restoring family honour through the Internet. In E. De Pauw, P. Ponsaers, K. van der Vijver, W. Bruggeman, & P. Deelman (Eds.). *Technology-led policing* (vol. 3, pp. 275–294). Maklu.

Levin, J., & Arluke, A. (1985). An exploratory analysis of sex differences in gossip. *Sex Roles, 12,* 281–286. https://doi.org/10.1007/BF00287594

Lowe, M., Khan, R., Thanzami, V., Barzy, M., & Karmaliani, R. (2018). Attitudes toward intimate partner "honor"-based violence in India, Iran, Malaysia and Pakistan. *Journal of Aggression, Conflict and Peace Research, 10*(4), 283–292. https://doi.org/10.1108/JACPR-09-2017-0324

Lowe, M., Khan, R., Thanzami, V., Barzy, M., & Karmaliani, R. (2021). Anti-gay "honor" abuse: A multinational attitudinal study of collectivist-versus individualist-orientated populations in Asia and England. *Journal of Interpersonal Violence, 36*(15–16), 7866–7885. https://doi.org/10.1177/0886260519838493

Mafura, C., & Charura, D. (2022). 'I then had 50 stitches in my arms… such damage to my own body': An Interpretative Phenomenological Analysis of Izzat trauma and self-harm experiences among UK women of South Asian heritage. *Counselling and Psychotherapy Research, 22*(2), 458–470. https://doi.org/10.1002/capr.12464

Magill, S. (2023). The "epidemic within the pandemic": meeting the needs of racially minoritised women experiencing domestic abuse during the Covid-19 pandemic. *Journal of Aggression, Conflict and Peace Research, 15*(3), 187–200. https://doi.org/10.1108/JACPR-05-2022-0717

Mayeda, D. T., Cho, S. R., & Vijaykumar, R. (2019). Honor-based violence and coercive control among Asian youth in Auckland, New Zealand. *Asian Journal of Women's Studies, 25*(2), 159–179. https://doi.org/10.1080/12259276.2019.1611010

McKenzie, K., Bhui, K., Nanchahal, K., & Blizard, B. (2008). Suicide rates in people of South Asian origin in England and Wales: 1993–2003. *The British Journal of Psychiatry, 193*(5), 406–409. https://doi.org/10.1192/bjp.bp.107.042598

McMahon, M., McGorrery, P. (2020). Criminalising Coercive Control: An Introduction. In M. McMahon & M. McGorrery (Eds.) *Criminalising Coercive Control.* Singapore: Springer. https://doi.org/10.1007/978-981-15-0653-6_1

Mendos, L. R., Botha, K., Leis, R. C., López de la Peña, E., Savlev, I., & Tan, D. (2020). *State-sponsored homophobia report. Global legislation overview update.* https://ilga.org/state-sponsored-homophobia-report/

Munaf, S. (2015). Parental acceptance and rejection - determinant of psychological adjustment and conduct of Pakistani adolescents. *Journal of Psychiatric Society, 12*(4), 26–28. http://www.jpps.com.pk/article/14578956659199-Parental%20Acceptance%20and%20Rejection%20as%20a%20Department%20of%20Psychological%20Adjustment%20and%20Conduct%20of%20Pakistani%20Adolescents%20.pdf

Newiss, G. (2005). A study of the characteristics of outstanding missing persons: implications for the development of police risk assessment. *Policing and society, 15*(2), 212–225. doi.org/10.1080/10439460500071655

Onal, A. (2012). *Honour killing. Stories of men who killed.* Saqi Books.

Özen-Dursun, B., Kaptan, S. K., Giles, S., Husain, N., & Panagioti, M. (2023). Understanding self-harm and suicidal behaviours in South Asian communities in the UK: systematic review and meta-synthesis. *BJPsych Open, 9*(3), e82. https://doi.org/10.1192/bjo.2023.63

Pall, S. & Kaur, S. (2021). *From Her, Kings are Born: Impact and prevalence of domestic and sexual violence in the Sikh/Punjabi Community*. Sikh Women's Aid. https://www.sikhwomensaid. org.uk/files/Sikh_Womens_Aid_From_Her_Kings_Are_Born.pdf

Patel, A. R., Prabhu, S., Sciarrino, N. A., Presseau, C., Smith, N. B., & Rozek, D. C. (2021). Gender-based violence and suicidal ideation among Indian women from slums: An examination of direct and indirect effects of depression, anxiety, and PTSD symptoms. *Psychological Trauma: Theory, Research, Practice, and Policy*, 13(6), 694–702. https://doi. org/10.1037/tra000099

Patel, S. P., & Gaw, A. C. (1996). Suicide among immigrants from the Indian subcontinent: A review. *Psychiatric Services*, 47(5), 517–521. https://doi.org/10.1176/ps.47.5.517

Patel, V., Ramasundarahettige, C., Vijayakumar, L., Thakur, J. S., Gajalakshmi, V., Gururaj, G., … & Million Death Study Collaborators. (2012). Suicide mortality in India: a nationally representative survey. *The Lancet*, 379(9834), 2343–2351. https://doi.org/10.1016/ S0140-6736(12)60606-0

Parekh, H., & Egan, V. (2021). Apostates as a hidden population of abuse victims. *Journal of Interpersonal Violence*, 36(23–24), 11681–11703. https://doi.org/10.1177%2F0886260519898428

Proudman, C. & Lloyd, F. (2023). The impact of COVID-19 on women and children in the UK who were victims of domestic abuse: a practitioner perspective. *Journal of Aggression, Conflict and Peace Research*, 15(3), 234–241. https://doi.org/10.1108/JACPR-07-2022-0734

Rahman, A. N. (2021). *Log Kya Kahenge (What Will People Say): Honour-Based Violence as a Response to Community Influenced Control and the Fear of Ostracization* (Maste's thesis, University of Calgary, Calgary, Canada). http://hdl.handle.net/1880/113062

Reiss, F. (2021). Child marriage in the United States: prevalence and implications. *Journal of Adolescent Health*, 69(6), S8–S10. https://doi.org/10.1016/j.jadohealth.2021.07.001

Ridley, K., Almond, L., Bafouni, N., & Qassim, A. (2023). 'Honour'-based abuse: A descriptive study of survivor, perpetrator, and abuse characteristics. *Journal of Investigative Psychology and Offender Profiling*, 20(1), 19–32. https://doi.org/10.1002/jip.1602

Rogers, M. (2017). Transphobic 'honour'-based abuse: a conceptual tool. *Sociology*, 51(2), 225–240. https://doi.org/10.1177/0038038515622907

Salter, M. (2014). Multi-perpetrator domestic violence. *Trauma, Violence, & Abuse*, 15(2), 102–112. https://doi.org/10.1177/1524838013511542

Sandhu, K. K., & Barrett, H. (2024). Girls just wanna have fun! South Asian women in the UK diaspora: Gradations of choice, agency, consent, and coercion. *Wome's Studies International Forum*, 102, 102859. https://doi.org/10.1016/j.wsif.2023.102859

Sandhu, K. K., & Barrett, H. R. (2020). "Should I stay, or should I go?": the experiences of, and choices available to women of south Asian heritage living in the UK when leaving a relationship of choice following intimate partner violence (IPV). *Social Sciences*, 9(9), 151. https://doi.org/10.3390/socsci9090151

Shahbazi, H., Sadeghi, M. A., & Panaghi, L. (2023). Dehumanization in female victims of intimate partner violence. *Journal of Injury & Violence Research*, 15(1), 83–95. https://doi. org/10.5249/jivr.v15i1.1676

Sharp, N. (2013). Missing from Discourse: South Asian Young Women and Sexual Exploitation. In: Melrose, M., Pearce, J. (Eds.). *Critical Perspectives on Child Sexual Exploitation and Related Trafficking*. Palgrave Macmillan. https://doi.org/10.1057/9781137294104_8

Sharp, N., (2010). *Forced marriage in the UK: a scoping study on the experience of women from Middle Eastern and North East African Communities*. Refuge. http://www.refuge.org.uk/ files/1001-Forced-Marriage-Middle-East-North-East-Africa.pdf

Sharp, N. (2015). Keeping it from the community. *Safer Communities, 14*(1), 56–66. https://doi.org/10.1108/SC-03-2015-0007

Shalev Greene, K., & Alys, L. (Eds.). (2016). *Missing persons: A handbook of research* (1st ed.). Routledge. https://doi.org/10.4324/9781315595603

Stark, E. (2023). *Coercive control: The entrapment of women in personal life* (2nd ed.). Oxford University Press. https://doi.org/10.1093/oso/9780197639986.001.0001

Steinke, C. (2013). Male asylum applicants who fear becoming the victims of honor killings: The case for gender equality. *City University of New York (CUNY) Law Review, 17,* 233–262. https://www.cunylawreview.org/wp-content/uploads/2014/09/CNY112.pdf

Tongsing, J. C. (2016). Domestic violence: Intersection of culture, gender and context. *Journal of Immigrant and Minority Health, 18*(2), 442–446. https://doi.org/10.1007/s10903-015-0193-1

Tongsing J., & Barn R. (2017). Intimate partner violence in South Asian communities: Exploring the notion of "shame" to promote understandings of migrant women's experiences. *International Social Work, 60*(3), 628–639. https://doi.org/10.1177/0020872816655868

Unchained at Last. (2024). *Forced and child marriage: Survivor stories.* https://www.unchainedatlast.org/forced-and-child-marriage-survivor-stories/

United Nations Development Programme. (2020). *Tackling Social Norms: A Game Changer for Gender Inequalities.* New York: United Nations Development Programme. https://www.undp.org/arab-states/publications/tackling-social-norms-game-changer-gender-inequalities

Vandello, J. (2016). Do we need a psychology of women in the Islamic world?. *Sex Roles, 75,* 623–629. https://doi.org/10.1007/s11199-016-0691-1

Way, N., & Rogers, L. O. (2017). Resistance to dehumanization during childhood and adolescence: A developmental and contextual process. In N. Budwig, E. Turil, & P. D. Zelazo (Eds.). *New perspectives on Human Development* (pp. 229–225). Cambridge University Press.

Yaakobi, E. (2021). Can cultural values eliminate ostracism distress?. *International Journal of Intercultural Relations, 80,* 231–241. https://doi.org/10.1016/j.ijintrel.2020.10.014

Perpetrators

6

In a prison interview, a 25-year-old man described his life after he was convicted and sentenced for first-degree murder in a so-called "honor" killing in Turkey:

> Seven years ago, I killed my mother and then gave myself up. ...
>
> I once heard someone say, in a film, that every murderer is actually the victim of the person he has murdered. We are murderers with our bodies but victims with our souls. That's why, while it is justice that punishes our bodies, it is our crime that punishes our souls. Which do you think is worse? Why do you think I did it? Because I'm very proud? Because my self-respect is so important to me? No, the main reason was to make the people who knew this secret hold their tongues, to shut their mouths. I did it so they would say, "even after so many years the man went ahead and killed his own mother, he cleansed his honour." You'll ask, has your honour been cleansed? No, it's much worse. I've become a murderer. I've murdered my own mother. I've lost my entire family and all of my friends. I don't know where I am headed in the next life...the most likely place for me in the next life is hell.
>
> (Onal, 2012, p. 30, p. 46)

Perpetrators of family violence, child abuse, and domestic homicide have been examined extensively in forensic psychology. Likewise, a substantial body of criminology research has explored the influence of patriarchal beliefs and culture on "honor" abuse, violence, and killings. Despite a rich psychological and criminological archive, this knowledge has not been synthesized into a theoretical model to explain the triggers, thoughts, reactions, conduct, and group

DOI: 10.4324/9781003299950-8

norms of people who endorse or perpetrate "honor" abuse, violence, and killings (Khan, 2018a).

Part 1 of this book explained why traditional research, theory, responses to, and interventions for family violence, child abuse, and domestic homicide perpetration are of little use in cases of "honor" abuse, violence, and killings. Chapter 1 explained that as explanatory models are Eurocentric, they fail to capture the antecedent, cognitive, emotional, behavioral, and social factors specific to this form of abuse, which mostly affects families who are not of Western heritage (Khan, 2018a; Kizilhan, 2019). This limitation has been caused (or compounded) by perpetrator myths and dual identities based on race/ethnicity stereotypes. As a result, research and intervention approaches with perpetrators overemphasize cultural aspects and underplay or overlook individual differences.

Each chapter in this book presents evidence that "honor" abuse, violence, and killings are distinct forms of family violence, child abuse, and domestic homicide. The unique features of which, as summarized in Chapter 3 (p. 3), are

> to protect and defend their honor, different types of abuse are committed, by one or more people (perpetrators) when they accuse a person or people (victims, most often women and girls) of behavior that has shamed them and damaged their public reputation.

One of the most distinctive aspects of "honor" abuse, violence, and killings perpetration is that any number of people can be involved in harming a victim, including immediate and extended family members. Although multiple perpetrators are reported in a sizable proportion of female domestic abuse victim cases, they are a distinct feature of "honor" abuse, violence, and killings. Specifically, Salter's (2014) review of peer-reviewed publications found two groups of girls and women were particularly vulnerable to multiple perpetrator domestic abuse. First, victims partnered with members of gangs and organized crime groups, and second, some victims with minoritized racial and ethnic identities, living in close-knit communities. A critical point of this review was multiple perpetration

> emerges from conditions of social and economic marginalization in which collective violence against girls and women serves as a means of establishing and protecting masculine honor and status [and] can include torturous or even homicidal levels of violence, and survivors have a range of mental, physical, and psychosocial problems.

(p. 104)

The following sections overview salient aspects of the victim-perpetrator relationship as a context for the three-phase model of "honor" abuse perpetration.

"Call it what you like, but...this is different" (Kaur, 2018)

Whether or not they share the same home or live in the same community, city, or country, a pattern to emerge from case studies is that perpetrators are almost always a female victim's family member and, in the case of male victims, the family of their spouse/partner (Dyer, 2015). Specifically, male relatives are most often perpetrators of "honor" abuse, violence, and killings (Hayes, Freilich, & Chermak, 2016). These include former/current husbands, fathers, and brothers, but also uncles, sons, and cousins (Chesler, 2009). Female relatives can also play a significant part in "honor" abuse, violence, and killings. For instance, mothers and mothers-in-law are most often reported, but also sisters, aunts, and female relatives' in-law (Elakkary et al., 2014;). In common with other cases of domestic abuse, violence, and homicide with female victims, perpetrators are often male current/ex-intimate partners. In a global estimate, 736 million women have been subjected to physical and/or sexual intimate partner violence at least once in their lives (Office for National Statistics, 2023; World Health Organization, 2021). Therefore, the primary role of a victim's father, brother, and/or mother is a distinguishing feature in the perpetration of "honor" abuse violence compared to other forms of domestic abuse, violence, and homicide.

The role of a victim's father is detailed in Chapters 4 and 5. The profile of a victim's brother and mother is overviewed in the following sections, with an outline of three high-profile "honor" abuse, violence, or killing cases involving brothers and mothers in Box 6.1.

Box 6.1   High-profile "honor" abuse, violence, or killing cases involving brothers and mothers

The three-phase model of "honor" abuse perpetration (Khan, 2024)
At the outset, it is important to note "honor" abuse, violence, and killings are no different from other forms of family violence, child abuse, and domestic homicide in that they can be inflicted on victims in many ways and to differing degrees. At one end of the spectrum is the subtle and insidious everyday monitoring of the victim's behavior. On the other extreme end is premeditated "honor" killing with tortuous violence and/or multiple perpetrators.

In the absence of an explanatory model of "honor" abuse perpetration, cases of "honor" abuse, violence, and killings have been particularly complex. Consider the UK police response to the "honor" abuse, violence, and killing of Banaz Mahmod, described in Chapter 2 (Box 2.1). Then, consider the social media post by Payzee Mahmod, Banaz's younger sister (Box 2.2), and her Preface at the start of this book. Next, consider the words of Nazir Afzal (2021), who, as the chief crown prosecutor for Banaz's case, noted this as particularly grueling:

> These cases resonate beyond the immediate family as we often deal with cases where significant members took part in the act; in the murder. And in the case of Banaz for instance, in addition substantial numbers of the community did not assist and support prosecutors. Instead, they supported the family members responsible for the killing. They really didn't care, and it showed. … We don't see this as domestic violence—it's beyond that. The murder or Banaz was so brutal that it was a clear warning to others; it was a way of saying "don't step out of line or this could be you."
>
> (Onal, 2012, p. 5)

These unique elements are captured in a new three-phase model of "honor" abuse perpetration (Khan, 2024), which, to be comprehensive, adaptable, and reliable, is based on five key principles: (1) to accurately account for existing patterns of perpetrator motivation and behavior, (2) to be consistent by drawing from related psychology and criminology theories and research, (3) to be broad in scope so it applies to a range of situations; (4) to simplify existing knowledge that is complex and disjointed, and (5) to be useful in research (by generating new observations and hypotheses) and in practice (for professionals in broad disciplines working with victims and perpetrators).

This explanatory model of "honor" abuse perpetration profiles the links between antecedent (triggers), cognitive (thoughts), emotional (reactions), behavioral (conduct), and social (group norms) elements of "honor" abuse, violence, and killings across three interlinked phases:

- **Phase 1**: to control and shape behavior
- **Phase 2**: to punish "dishonorable" behavior
- **Phase 3**: to protect perpetrators and blame victims

Many cases of "honor" abuse do not escalate beyond Phase 1, where the control and shaping of behavior may be present but subtle and is often not recognized as harmful. If cases enter Phase 2, where punishment is coercive or verbal scolding but not consistently harsh or physical, again, this may not be viewed by observers as unharmful. The new three-phase model of "honor" abuse perpetration (Khan, 2024) is presented in Figure 6.1 and overviewed in detail in the following sections.

Rukhsana Naz was a 19-year-old pregnant mother of two when she was murdered in an "honor" killing in England. Rukhsana's mother and her 21-year-old brother were found guilty of her murder and sentenced to life in prison in 1999. Her 18-year-old brother was acquitted. The key prosecution witnesses were Rukhsana's sister and her younger brother's girlfriend (Naz, R v England and Wales Court of Appeal, 2000). Although Rukhsana's mother and brothers gave conflicting accounts of what happened, police investigations revealed her mother, who considered Rukhsana's pregnancy to be dishonorable, held her legs down and instructed her older son to strangle her to death with a plastic flex. Her younger brother (who claimed to be a helpless witness to his sister's murder) assisted in the disposal of Rukhsana's body, which was dumped some miles away in a field (Dyer, 2015; Khan, 2018b).

Afshan Azad is a British actress best known for her role as Padma Patil in the Harry Potter film series. When she was 22 years old, Afshan's father and 28-year-old brother attacked her in her bedroom, angered by her relationship with a young Hindu man. They appeared in Magistrates' Court in England charged with threatening to kill her. In a "prolonged and nasty" attack, Afshan's brother shouted at her, grabbed her hair, then threw her across the room. When she began to cry and asked him to stop, he punched her in the back and head with clenched fists. He pushed Afshan onto their father's bed and shouted, "Sort your daughter out! She's a slag," before throttling her by the neck (Dyer, 2015, p. 22). After the assault, Afshan's father suggested she be sent to Bangladesh to be married. Her mother called her a "prostitute." The prosecution accepted Afshan's brother's guilty plea to assault occasioning actual bodily harm, and in 2011, he was imprisoned for six months. Afshan wrote to the judge in the case to ask for her brother to be freed so she could be reconciled with her family (Bhatti, 2011).

Qandeel Baloch, a social media star dubbed the "Kim Kardashian of Pakistan," was strangled to death by her brother while asleep in her parents' house in 2016. He claimed she had brought shame on the family. She was 26 years old. In 2019, Baloch's brother was sentenced to life imprisonment for her murder (Ahmed, 2019). Pakistan passed legislation in 2016 mandating life in prison for "honor" killings to close a loophole that allowed families to pardon the crime. In 2022, he was acquitted after a judge ruled the crime was not an "honor" killing and, in line with Pakistan's other laws on murder, his mother was still allowed to grant his freedom. His mother told reporters, "I am thankful to the court, which ordered the release of my son at our request." She added, "[W]e are still sad for our daughter's loss" (*Qandeel Baloch: Court acquits brother of Pakistan star's murder*, 2022).

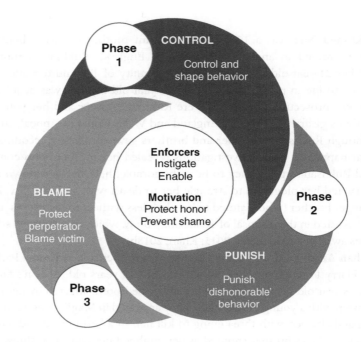

Figure 6.1 The three-phase model of "honor" abuse perpetration

Brothers

Although sibling conflict is common, some of these relationships are characterized by one-directional aggression and violence, expressed as physical, sexual, psychological, and/or financial abuse (Khan & Brewer, 2021). Most sibling violence studies are conducted with families in individualist cultures, where prevalence estimates between 70% and 96% are some of the highest in family violence research (Khan & Rogers, 2015). However, siblicide rates are low and range between 1% and 8% (Khan, 2017; Walsh & Krienert, 2014).

Despite substantial brother-to-sister power and control dynamics in families that endorse masculine honor codes, few studies have examined sibling relationships in collectivist honor cultures (Perkins & Rai, 2023; Purkayastha, 2000; Relva & Khan, 2021). Fewer studies have examined "honor" abuse, violence, and killings by brothers in this cultural context, where brother-sister relationships are described as "intimate and symbiotic but fragile" (Bhanbhro, 2021, p. 2). In these relationships, a brother's power and authority over his sister can extend beyond their home and can be socially accepted and legally authorized. As noted in Chapter 4, until 1981, the Italian penal code provided reduced sentences for male relatives who killed their adulterous wives, daughters, or sisters (De Cristofaro, 2018).

In the United Kingdom, honor abuse and violence are most frequently reported in South Asian families (Dyer, 2015; Khan, Morris, & Mulongo, 2024; Khan, Saleem, & Lowe, 2018). A study of 16- to 25-year-old British Pakistanis found physical abuse by siblings tended to be overlooked by parents (Irfan & Cowburn, 2004). Normalization of sibling violence is common in many families, regardless of their ethnic or cultural heritage (Khan & Rogers, 2015). However, this study found a power imbalance in favor of brothers, which elevated their social position over sisters, regardless of age, and they were expected to exert authority over them, act as disciplinarians, and take over the father's role without being challenged by either parent. This pattern is illustrated in the cases outlined in Box 6.1 and in "honor" killing prevalence data presented in Chapter 4. For instance, in an analysis of 4,070 "honor" killings in Pakistan, the killer in nearly a quarter of these cases (22%; N = 926) was a female victim's brother (Bhanbhro, 2021). In these cases, brothers often played a part in policing their sister's behavior and took a lead role in punishing them—either psychological or physical abuse—or were involved in killing her. Likewise, a study of "honor" killings in Jordan found brothers accounted for 60% of perpetrators (Kulwicki, 2002). In the 89 homicide cases reviewed, a male relative of the female victim, primarily the brother, committed the murders, claiming their sister had violated the family's "honor." Other researchers propose a victim's brother (often the youngest) may be elected by the rest of the family to commit an "honor" killing—if they are under the age of full criminal responsibility, this may result in a lesser sentence (Elakkary et al., 2014; Oberwittler & Kasselt, 2014).

Mothers

Understanding perpetrators of any form of family violence, child abuse, and domestic homicide challenges the sentimental view of family life—that of an adored child and playful siblings raised by a nurturing mother and protective father, flourishing in a healthy and safe home environment, valued by relatives. This simplified view obscures the harm inflicted by different family members. For instance, statistics show that in the United States, around 338,747 perpetrators of child abuse were a victim's biological parent, and a further 30,033 perpetrators were a victim's relative (Statista, 2023a). Also, more child abuse perpetrators were women (233,918) than were men (213,672) (Statista, 2023b). Reviews of maternal filicide (or child murder by mothers) have identified a range of motives (Resnick, 2016; Friedman & Resnick, 2007). This includes *fatal maltreatment filicide* (from abuse or neglect), *unwanted child filicide* (when a child is viewed as a hindrance), and, most rare, *spouse revenge filicide* (when a child is killed with the intention of emotionally harming that child's father). In cases of "honor" abuse, violence, and killings, the main motivation for harmdoing is a victim's apparent "shame" and "dishonor."

Research rarely examines the unsettling nature of love in abusive relationships (Pocock, Jackson, & Bradbury-Jones, 2020; Stead, Brewer, Gardner, & Khan, 2022). In cases of "honor" abuse, violence, and killings, this may be salient, as studies note an accusation of "dishonor" and "shame" can "override the emotional desire to love and protect family members and friends. It is not uncommon for loved ones to turn their backs on vulnerable girls and women, refusing to defend them or to offer them refuge" (Begum, Khan, Brewer, & Hall, 2020, p. 2). Insights from evolutionary perspectives indicate maternal love did not evolve to be unconditional, inevitable, or altruistic, regardless of the circumstance. Instead, women's maternal emotions (and the behaviors influenced by those emotions) evolved to be sensitive to a host of contextual factors (Wren, Launer, Music, Reiss, & Swanepoel, 2021).

Studies have examined the salient role that female relatives play, particularly mothers and mothers-in-law, in cases of "honor" abuse, violence, and killings. A study of 100 cases and 15 interviews with specialist officers in a UK police force found mothers were the "driving forces" in "honor" abuse cases and had perpetrated almost two-thirds of all cases involving women. The study author stated, "[M]others play fundamental, indeed 'massive' role in perpetrating honor abuse against daughters. Mothers inflict violence, sometimes with an intention to induce an abortion; they inflict hard psychological abuse and condone the violence inflicted by other male relatives, mainly sons" (Aplin, 2017, p. 1).

In an examination of 1,500 case files of female honor abuse perpetrators in the United Kingdom, 5% involved a female acting alone, while the remaining 95% of cases involved one or more other perpetrators (Bates, 2018). In these cases, female perpetrators were a victim's mother (52%) or relatives-in-law (mother, sister, or aunt) (40%), an ex-wife/girlfriend (9%), or sisters or aunts (5%). The type of abuse differed with mothers more commonly using controlling behavior and emotional manipulation (e.g., crying or pleading with victims not to shame them and threatening to self-harm or kill themselves). In contrast, mothers-in-law were more likely to entrap victims, forcing them into domestic servitude and using physical violence (e.g., slapping, pushing, beating). The study identified three different types of roles these women adopted. Specifically: (1) controller—taking a lead role in the abuse, (2) collaborators—actively colluding in abusing the victim but playing a specific role (e.g., threats to harm themselves or policing a victim's whereabouts), and (3) coerced—whereby the female preparator seemed to be a victim of coercion or intimidation themselves, for example, domestic abuse inflicted by her husband.

A common query in cases of "honor" abuse, violence, and killings is for observers to ask why a mother did not protect her daughter from an abusive father or son. And why, instead, the victim's mother protected the abusive husband or son, as in the cases of Afshan Azad and Qandeel Baloch outlined in Box 6.1. Indeed, why do some women from collectivist honor cultures shame and harm other females in the name of so-called "honor", when they too are at risk of that same cruelty and maltreatment? As outlined in Chapter 3, one explanation of this victim-blame paradox (Khan, 2018b) is the Just World hypothesis, which asserts that, as the world is presumed by many to be a fair and just place, people implicitly believe a victim of "honor" abuse, violence, or killing must have acted in a way to deserve it (Khan, 2018b). Another explanation is patriarchal bargaining (Kandiyoti, 1988). From this view, a female's social position is shaped by, and constrained within, an overwhelming vacuum of patriarchal control. In this way, girls and women face a difficult choice of protecting themselves or protecting someone else. They must decide to either defend themselves or defend another female.

There is little understanding of this complex cognitive decision-making in academic research and professional practice. This is because traditional explanatory models of family violence, child abuse, and domestic homicide are based on perpetrator-victim dynamics that are vastly different from most cases of "honor" abuse, violence, and killings. In the former case, there is a focus on one main perpetrator (e.g., a current or ex-intimate partner). Further, if other family members are aware of the abuse, generally, they disapprove of the perpetrator and their actions, and the victim is defended, protected, and supported. In the latter case, perpetrators can be younger, older, or same-aged relatives or peers either in a victim's immediate or extended family or members of their local/ wider community, including overseas in countries of heritage. Anyone of the people in this network may be involved in controlling or punishing a victim, including those who do not wish to cause the victim harm.

Enforcer network

"Honor" based abuse is a powerful means of behavioral control that functions to ensure people conduct themselves in a way considered to be socially acceptable. In tight-knit communities in honor cultures, this system of social control is effective, as it is maintained by any number of enforcers who form a powerful, hidden network.

Enforcers are any number of people who, in different roles, act separately or together and are motivated to protect the public reputation of their family by ensuring each family member behaves in a way deemed honorable. In close-knit communities, characterized by families strictly adhering to honor codes, a powerful and hidden network is formed in which immediate and extended family members, across numerous communities, share the responsibility of maintaining their own and each other's honorable reputation.

Enforcers use a range of methods to control each other's behavior (to align with honor codes) and for punishment (when behavior does not align with honor codes). As described in Chapter 5 and shown in Figures 5 and 6, honor codes are rigidly gendered and emphasize female chastity. Specifically, boys and men maintain their own and their family's honor using hypermasculine behavior to coerce, control, and punish, if need be, to guard female relatives' chastity. Girls and women maintain their own and their family's honorable status by guarding their own virginity and fidelity. Girls are expected to obey the wishes of their fathers and brothers, and married women are expected to be submissive to their husbands (Khan, 2018b; Vandello, 2016). There are two main roles enforcers may adopt in their network, whether working separately or together.

Instigators

- Instigators are network ringleaders who take a lead role in monitoring and judging whether honor codes are followed by other people, most often their own family members or intimate partners.
- Instigators initiate punishments for people judged, they claim, to have acted with "dishonor" and "shame," thus damaging their family's public reputation.

Enablers

- Enablers contribute to the network by enforcing an instigator's actions (i.e., monitoring, judging, reporting, punishing others).
- Enablers might be reluctant to support an instigator, and some may be coerced or threatened into doing so under duress. In this way, some enablers can be viewed as unwilling enablers, and in some cases, they are secondary victims.

The instigator and enabler roles can overlap or merge, thereby increasing the strength of the enforcer network. In this way, instigators and enablers are able to monitor real-life and online behavior in three key phases.

- During Phase 1, children are socialized to behave in a way that aligns with gendered honor codes.
- During Phase 2, children and adults are punished if their behavior is deemed to fall out of line with gendered honor codes.

- During Phase 3, if external intervention is taking place (e.g., if police or welfare services are alerted), instigators are protected, and victims are blamed.

One view is that families in close-knit communities in collectivist culture are not abusive to start with. Instead, when young people break the rigid gender honor codes, the authoritarian family and community response is one of strict intolerance without negotiation, which leads to a critical point of no return (Irfan & Cowburn, 2004).

Phase 1: control and shape behavior

Motivation

During Phase 1, enforcers' motivations are twofold. First, to encourage girls to follow female honor codes by guarding their chastity and accepting their fathers' and/or brothers' authority. Second, to encourage boys to follow male honor codes using hypermasculine behaviors to guard the chastity of female relatives. This is detailed in Chapter 3 and illustrated in Chapter 5 in Figures 5.1 and 5.2. Both girls and boys are expected to publicly demonstrate these traits so that others can observe them.

It is long established that in all societies across the world, children learn social norms and expectations via observation, vicarious reinforcement, and punishment, while the rigidity of gendered norms can vary across cultures. Children's knowledge of gender norms increases with age (through the preschool years), while the possibility that someone can violate gender norms increases through middle childhood (Blakemore, 2003).

Due to early socialization, it is instilled in children to associate rigidly gendered behavior with family honor, so it forms a core part of children's personal identity (Mahapatra & Murugan, 2024). From childhood to adolescence and then adulthood, girls and boys learn to conduct themselves in a way deemed to be honorable so as not to shame their families. Beginning in childhood, instigators and enablers, either separately or collectively, observe, monitor, and curb the behavior of girls and boys in their families and local community to ensure they behave in line with socially approved female and male honor codes (Khan, 2018b; Vandello, 2016).

- Girls are expected to be nonsexual, demonstrated by a modest appearance and submissive behavior. Boys are expected to be tough, taking on a parentified role by policing girls' behavior, reprimanding girls directly, and then reporting to their parents if their conduct is judged to be out of line with gendered social expectations (Irfan & Cowburn, 2004).

- A boy's behavior, too, can be judged harshly if he is also deemed not to be behaving in line with male-gendered codes. For instance, if a brother does not appropriately monitor, reprimand, or report his sister's behavior (Bhanbhro, 2023). Also, if his behavior is not overtly heterosexual (Idriss, 2020, 2022).

Methods

Instigators and enablers, separately or collectively, use a range of behaviors to monitor and pressure girls and boys to ensure they adhere to gendered honor codes.

- Instigators are more likely to be adult or adolescent males who are immediate family members (i.e., fathers, sons, and brothers) (Bhanbhro, 2021). Mothers can also take primary instigator roles (Aplin, 2017; Bates, 2018).
- Instigators are likely to use a range of tactics to ensure compliance from daughters and sons in childhood, including coercive and controlling behavior, victim blaming, and/or physical violence. Harsh discipline as a form of punishment to curb behavior is likely to occur in families who rigidly observe honor codes (Irfan & Cowburn, 2004).
- Enablers may be other male and female relatives (nephews, aunts, cousins, and in-laws), some of whom are secondary victims forced to comply due to threats or coercion. The network of enablers in the community may live locally, in the same city or country, or overseas in the family's country of heritage (Khan, 2018b).
- Enablers are likely to use a range of tactics to monitor, scrutinize, and threaten to report on girls' and women's behavior, in person or online (Janssen, Sanberg, & van der Sluis, 2011; Lowe, Khan, Thanzami, Barzy, & Karmaliani, 2021). Enablers may also monitor male family/community members to ensure they are policing female relative's behavior.
- Enablers, like instigators, may use coercive and controlling behavior and victim blaming. However, they may be more likely to engage in gossip to slur, insult, and shame female targets accused of behaving out of line with the female honor code (Awwad, 2001; Cooney, 2014). This is described in detail in Chapter 5 in relation to coercive control—"murder by language."

Psychological processes

- *Impact on girls*: As described in Chapter 5, an oppressive home life characterized by monitoring, controlling, and scrutiny of behavior without a physical or psychological release from the situation can lead to a sense of guilt, shame, dehumanization, and self-dehumanization (Sandhu & Barrett, 2020, 2024; Way & Rogers, 2017; Shahbazi, Sadeghi, & Panaghi, 2023).
- *Impact on boys*: Machismo and male superiority are instilled in boys at a young age, who are encouraged, independently and collectively, to monitor their sisters' behavior when parents and other elders are absent. Consequently, boys will be socialized to adhere to the hypermasculine norms, to maintain masculine honor codes.
- *Impact on instigators and enablers*: Girls may undergo a process of dehumanization and self-dehumanization, making it easier to objectify and control them. This enables instigators and enablers to justify the removal of female autonomy and maltreatment. In tight-knit communities in honor cultures, these demeaning beliefs about girls and women are presented as social norms and perpetuated to form a cultural norm in which personalized aggression against females is tolerated if used to protect family honor. Individuals who question rigid gendered norms are viewed as marginalized outsiders. As challenging or not following gendered norms could be viewed as an honor-related failure, male instigators and enablers may experience psychological distress, for instance, anxiety or depression (Osterman & Brown, 2011). Males in this context could be less likely to seek support for this distress due to the belief that not following a masculine honor code (e.g., viewing help-seeking as a nonmasculine trait) may threaten their public reputation.

Phase 2: punish "dishonorable" behavior

Motivation

If a girl or woman is observed (or it is implied by gossip) behaving in a way that is perceived to break the female honor code, this challenges the public reputation of her family. Instigators and enablers, either separately or collectively, may judge and then warn her to redress her behavior. In some cases, she may be punished. See Box 5.1 in Chapter 5 for motivations and types of "honor" abuse and violence: symbolic, social, psychological, and physical.

Instigators often take the lead in physical chastisement. Victims can be warned or punished for a range of behaviors deemed to break an honor code

---

Box 6.2 Examples of "dishonorable" behavior perceived to break honor codes

- Loss of virginity outside marriage
- Extramarital relationship
- Rebelling against traditional forms of behavior, dress, or occupation
- Insulting a family member
- Seeking a divorce
- Rejecting or leaving a forced marriage
- Homosexuality and/or transgender identity
- Refusing to take part in "honor" abuse, violence, or killing against another person as an instigator or enabler

---

(Khan, 2018b), as shown in Box 6.2. Significantly, while females are likely to be punished for any one of the behaviors in the list, males are more likely to be punished for the last three examples (e.g., rejecting/leaving a forced marriage, homosexuality, trans identity, refusing to be an instigator or enabler). Although rare, in extreme cases, male instigators have punished female relatives for being victims of sexual assault and rape due to the belief that female chastity is the ultimate expression of family honor (see Alsabti, 2016, pp. 459–460). Fischbach and Herbert (1997, p. 1162) state, "Where virginity determines the woman's worth, the stigma of rape is particularly devastating."

If family or community members raise concern about a victim's situation or challenge rigid gender norms, they, too, risk punishment by instigators and/or enablers to bring them back in line with collective thinking and practices. "Family members who know the truth about an 'honour' killing are often too scared to cooperate with the authorities, or actually collude in the crime" (Smith, 2011). Another salient feature is that the desire to punish a victim and those who attempt to help her can span over a long period of time (Alam et al., 2023).

Methods

- Male instigators and enablers will be motivated due to rigid gender socialization to act tough and maintain control over females and males accused of transgressing honor codes by disciplining them and those who defend the victims.

- Female instigators and enablers (in a victim-blame paradox, Khan, 2018b; or patriarchal bargaining, Kandiyoti, 1988) may endorse/condone the abuse committed by female and male instigators and enablers. They may use physical means if deemed necessary, but most often, they publicly shame the victim using gossip, slurs, and harassment to accuse her of dishonoring and shaming her family. This has been referred to as "hard psychological abuse" (Aplin, 2017), the power of which is reflected in the coining of the phrase "murder by language" (Chesler, 2015).

- The types of behaviors used to reprimand the victim range from verbal threats, intimidation, and harassment to premeditated physical violence, the most extreme of which is premeditated killing, termed "execution by family" (Cooney, 2014). Punishment methods are characterized by public display and excessive force. Even when instigators and enablers are pressured into punishing a victim (under duress of being chastised or ostracized if they do not), their reputation may be enhanced for restoring family "honor" by punishing the victim. Once shame threatens the family's honor, it becomes a concern of the entire community, and not just the family, so the victim's punishment is broadcast, for example, via gossip across the network (Awwad, 2001). Excessive force is evident in many cases of "honor" killing, in which instigators may use overkill—a term forensic pathologists use to describe the infliction of massive injuries that by far exceed the extent necessary to cause the victim's death (Solarino, Punzi, Di Vella, Carabellese, & Catanesi, 2019). Although "honor" killings are not common compared to other forms of domestic homicide, they sometimes feature torture and overkill. Of note is the belief men must respond aggressively to perceived threats or insults to be considered masculine and respectable (i.e., masculine honor ideology), which is a strong, direct predictor of aggression and is related to everyday sadism (Benemann, McCartin, Russell, Cash, & King, 2023). Overkill is evident in the "honor" killing of Sumandeep Kaur, a 20-year-old woman by her father. He dragged Sumandeep by her hair, attacked her with a sharp weapon, and then left her dead body on a railway line. He later paraded her body on a motorbike through their village. When in police custody, he was reported to say: "I killed my daughter because she stayed outside with somebody. I killed her because of my pride, and this will also serve as a lesson to other girls" (Jha, 2023). In another example of overkill, Asifa Rashid, an 18-year-old woman who challenged her family's wishes regarding her marriage, was attacked by her 24-year-old brother. He reportedly used a sharp-edged weapon to behead her. He carried a blood-soaked sack with her head inside through the local streets to a police station, where he was arrested (Chakraborty, 2023).

Psychological processes

- *Impact on instigators and enablers*: As described in Chapter 5, instigators and enablers may be psychologically and socially motivated to punish the victim and the victim's supporters. Those who refuse or resist punishing a victim may risk "social death" and be ostracized from their families and communities (Chhina, 2017). Doğan (2018, p. 1249) states that "losing social identity, personal value, or withdrawing from the community is not voluntary and does not result from personal autonomy or choice. It results from alienation, social exclusion, and disapproval that the person in question or any person does not want to experience at all."
- As family honor and close-knit community cohesiveness are linked to controlling behavior and punishment for breaking strict gendered honor codes, this may cause individual family or community members to experience cognitive dissonance—the mental toil of conflicting beliefs, values, or attitudes. In turn, this may lead to a sense of disequilibrium—a cognitive imbalance when encountering information that requires the development of a new schema or the modification of existing schema—that is, a pattern of thinking and behavior that people use to interpret the world. The dehumanization of victims plays a part in restoring equilibrium (Smith, 2011). In this way, core beliefs are formulated about the self, others, and environment, leading to normalization and desensitization of the subjugation of girls and women.

Phase 3: protect perpetrators, blame victim

Motivation

In Phase 3, if intervention has taken place during Phase 1 or Phase 2 (e.g., police or welfare services are alerted), enablers separately or collectively protect instigators by minimizing or justifying their harmful actions while blaming the victim. That is, to maintain the status quo, enablers defend the instigator and downplay the harm inflicted on the victim.

Methods

- Enablers may use a range of evasive tactics to minimize the harm caused to a victim by an instigator's controlling behavior (in Phase 1) or punishment (in Phase 2) when this is questioned by people who are not in the enabler network or is reported to external authorities who might intervene. As described in Chapter 3, in honor cultures characterized by rigid gender roles, protection of the group ("we") surpasses the needs and beliefs of individuals ("I"), and this is reinforced due to the strong bonds with immediate and extended family, as well as their community.

- To protect the instigator and enabler network, protection strategies used may include making misleading reports, false facts that incriminate the victim and those defending them, lying about the instigator's whereabouts, sheltering the instigator so they can evade arrest, hiding/destroying evidence, claiming the victim had instigated any violence witnessed, and/or defending the instigator's actions in a way that reframes them as a victim. These actions align with the five techniques in Neutralization Theory, which has been used to explain how "honor" abuse perpetrators justify their actions and overcome feelings of guilt and shame for doing so (van Baak, Hayes, Freilich, & Chermak, 2018; Doğan, 2014a, b, 2016). These are denial of responsibility, denial of injury, denial of victim, condemnation of condemners, and appeal to higher loyalties. Also, perpetrators, who are most often men, "typically minimize, excuse, deny, or justify their use of violence against women, and seek to neutralize their violence by minimizing its effect and degree" (Regis-Moura, Ferreira, Bonfá-Araujo, & Iglesias, 2022). Similarly, as the eight mechanisms (or "psychosocial maneuvers") in the Moral Disengagement Model (Bandura, 2002) explain, disengagement from abusive conduct can be achieved by reframing inexcusable actions or by minimizing its effects and blaming victims. In this way, disengagement focuses on redefining harmful conduct as honorable by moral justification, exonerating social comparison, and sanitizing language. This disengagement was discussed in Chapter 3 and outlined in Table 3.1 in Abu-Odeh's (1997) analysis of violence against women, which found that "honor" crimes were based on the notion of justification.
- Victims, via intensive coercion and fear of (or actual) punishment, may also be involved in protecting the instigator and enablers. They may publicly forgive them or claim that an abuser's behavior has changed since they were arrested or brought to trial, and they make a plea for leniency and/or self-blame. This is illustrated in the case of Afshan Azad (see Box 6.1).

Psychological processes

Impact on enablers: As victims have been controlled and objectified (or dehumanized) from childhood (Phases 1 and 2), it becomes easier for their maltreatment to be justified, and so there is less cognitive dissonance. Even when enablers sympathize or empathize with a victim, the objectification (or dehumanization) process has instilled a collective belief that underpins the social norm that one "lesser" person can be expendable for the sake of the "greater" good.

There is some evidence to suggest that when instigators or enablers have been forced to be involved in Phase 3, this has a deleterious effect on them. Men's psychological well-being in cultures of honor is associated with an increased risk of suicide and being less likely to seek mental health care and resources (Gul, Cross, & Uskul, 2021). In three studies of "honor" killing by Doğan, one female and two males attempted to end their lives by suicide after they committed a murder but were prevented from doing so. One male perpetrator attempted suicide before the murder (Doğan, 2014a, b, 2016).

End of chapter reflections

This new three-phase model of "honor" abuse perpetration (Khan, 2024) shows how this powerful and hidden enforcer network is led by dominant instigators and maintained by willing enablers. Some enablers who contribute to enforcing the network under duress or by violence may be regarded as secondary victims.

The enforcer network also contributes to how individuals, families, and communities in honor cultures are viewed by those not in the network. As detailed in Chapter 3, perpetrators may justify their abusive conduct based on race, cultural, or religious grounds, leading to the weaponization of "honor" abuse, violence, and killings to demonize Middle Eastern and South Asian families of the Islamic faith. Despite convoluted reasoning and victim-blame rhetoric of enforcers who commit or endorse "honor" abuse, violence, or killing, it is not a legal punishment. In fact, the "loss of honor" defense, which some enforcers have used to justify violence or murder, is not applicable in any court of law around the world (Singh & Bhandari, 2021).

Part 1 of this book highlighted that research on perpetrators of "honor" abuse, violence, and killings is rare. Further, when studies are conducted, they almost always focus on demographic factors, while psychosocial factors are seldom, if ever, considered. On the other hand, substantial research has been conducted on perpetrators of other forms of family violence, child abuse, and domestic homicide, and these explore a wide range of psychosocial factors, such as interpersonal, intrapersonal, biological, disinhibitory behavior, and psychopathology. It is clear that current explanations for "honor" abuse, violence, and killings have been culturized not simply because they are more commonly reported in non-Western families but because individual differences and psychosocial explanations are not even considered.

The three-phase model of "honor" abuse perpetration presented in this chapter highlighted a range of factors that research studies should investigate. These include the influence of cognitive, emotional, behavioral, and social factors as antecedents to "honor" abuse, violence, and killings. These include psychopathy, hypermasculinity, and everyday sadism in relation to instigators. In relation to crime detail, it may be of value to examine why instigators and enablers may be motivated to commit overkill. In willing enablers, there is a scope to examine the influence of extreme conformity and related personality factors. And in those who do not conform with the enabler network, investigations into why they were motivated to risk being ostracized from family and community and suffering a "social death" are needed.

References

Abu-Odeh, L. (1997). Comparatively speaking: the honor of the east and the passion of the west. *Utah Law Review, 1997*(2), 287–308. https://heinonline.org/HOL/LandingPage?handle=hein.journals/utahlr1997&div=23&id=&page=

Afzal, N. (2021). *The prosecutor*. Ebury Press.

Ahmed, S. (2019). The honor killing of Qandeel Baloch: Visibility through social media and its repercussions. In K. Zaleski, A. Enrile, X. Wang, & E. L. Weiss (Eds.), *Wome's journey to empowerment in the 21st century: A transnational feminist analysis of women's lives in modern times* (pp. 135–146). Oxford University Press. https://doi.org/10.1093/oso/9780190927097.003.0008

Alam, A., Khan, R., Graham-Kevan, N. (2023). Family "honor" killings. In T. K. Shackelford (Ed.), *Encyclopedia of Domestic Violence* (pp. 1–4). Springer. https://doi.org/10.1007/978-3-030-85493-5_528-1

Alsabti, S. (2016). Honor killing and the indigenous peoples: Cultural right or human right violation. *Denver Journal of International Law & Policy, 45*(4), 457–470. https://digitalcommons.du.edu/cgi/viewcontent.cgi?article=1020&context=djilp

Aplin, R. (2017). Exploring the role of mothers in 'honour' based abuse perpetration and the impact on the policing response. *Women's Studies International Forum, 60*, 1–10. https://doi.org/10.1016/j.wsif.2016.10.007

Awwad, A. M. (2001). Gossip, scandal, shame and honor killing: A case for social constructionism and hegemonic discourse. *Social Thought & Research*, 39–52. https://www.jstor.org/stable/23250074

Bandura A. (2002). Selective moral disengagement in the exercise of moral agency. *Journal of Moral Education, 31*(2), 101–119. https://doi.org/10.1080/0305724022014322

Bates, L. (2018). Females perpetrating honour-based abuse: controllers, collaborators or coerced?. *Journal of Aggression, Conflict and Peace Research, 10*(4), 293–303. https://doi.org/10.1108/JACPR-01-2018-0341

Begum, R., Khan, R., Brewer, G., & Hall, B. (2020). "They will keep seeing young women murdered by men. Enough is enough-we have seen too many women lose their lives". lessons for professionals working with victims of 'honour' abuse and violence. *Genealogy, 4*(3), 1–12. https://doi.org/10.3390/genealogy4030069

Benemann, H., McCartin, H., Russell, T., Cash, D., & King, A. (2023). Sadistic masculinity: Masculine honor ideology mediates sadism and aggression. *Personality and Individual Differences, 206*, 112118. https://doi.org/10.1016/j.paid.2023.112118

Bhanbhro, S. (2021). Brothers who kill: murders of sisters for the sake of family honour in Pakistan. In A. Buchanan., & A. Rotkirch. (Eds). *Brothers and Sisters*. Palgrave Macmillan. https://doi.org/10.1007/978-3-030-55985-417

Bhanbhro, S. (2023). Honour Crimes. In P. Ali, & M. M. Rogers (Eds.), *Gender-Based Violence: A Comprehensive Guide* (pp. 285–297). Springer. https://doi.org/10.1007/978-3-031-05640-6

Bhatti, A. (2011, January 27). Broken family values. *The Guardian*. https://www.theguardian.com/commentisfree/belief/2011/jan/27/afshan-azad-assault-case

Blakemore, J. E. O. (2003). Childre's beliefs about violating gender norms: Boys shouldn't look like girls, and girls shouldn't act like boys. *Sex Roles, 48*, 411–419. https://doi.org/10.1023/A:1023574427720

Chakraborty, P. (2023, July 21). Man beheads his sister in UP's Barabanki district; takes 'severed head' in sack to police station. *The Times of India*. https://timesofindia.indiatimes.com/city/lucknow/man-beheads-his-sister-in-ups-barabanki-district-takes-severed-head-in-sack-to-police-station/articleshow/102013613.cms?from=mdr

Chesler, P. (2009). Are Honor Killings Simply Domestic Violence? *Middle East Quarterly, 16*(2), 61–69. https://www.meforum.org/2067/are-honor-killings-simply-domestic-violence

Chesler, P. (2015). When women commit honor killings. *Middle East Quarterly, 22*(4). https://www.meforum.org/5477/when-women-commit-honor-killings?source=post_page

Chhina, R. (2017). *An exploration of the experiences of challenging Izzat among six South Asian women City*. University of London. http://yorksj.idm.oclc.org/login?url=https://search.ebscohost.com/login.aspx?direct=true&db=edsble&AN=edsble.738450&site=eds-live&scope=site

Cooney, M. (2014). Death by family: Honor violence as punishment. *Punishment & Society, 16*(4), 406–427. https://doi.org/10.1177/1462474514539537

De Cristofaro, E. (2018). The crime of honor: an Italian story. *Historia et ius, 14*, 1–12. http://www.historiaetius.eu/uploads/5/9/4/8/5948821/14_15_de_cristofaro.pdf

Doğan, R. (2014a). The profiles of victims, perpetrators, and unfounded beliefs in honor killings in Turkey. *Homicide Studies, 18*(4), 389–416. https://doi.org/10.1177/1088767914538637

Doğan, R. (2014b). Different cultural understandings of honor that inspire killing: An inquiry into the defendant's perspective. *Homicide Studies, 18*(4), 363–388. https://doi.org/10.1177/1088767914526717

Doğan, R. (2016). The dynamics of honor killings and the perpetrators' experiences. *Homicide Studies, 20*(1), 53–57. https://doi.org/10.1177/1088767914563389

Doğan, R. (2018). Do women really kill for honor? conceptualizing women's involvement in honor killings. *Deviant Behavior, 39*(10), 1247–1266. https://doi.org/10.1080/01639625.2017.1420454

Dyer, E. (2015). *'Honour' killings in the UK*. Henry Jackson Society. https://henryjacksonsociety.org/wp-content/uploads/2015/01/Honour-Killings-in-the-UK.pdf

Elakkary, S., Franke, B., Shokri, D., Hartwig, S., Tsokos, M., & Püschel, K. (2014). Honor crimes: Review and proposed definition. *Forensic Science, Medicine, and Pathology, 10*, 76–82. https://doi.org/10.1007/s12024-013-9455-1

Fischbach, R. L., & Herbert, B. (1997). Domestic violence and mental health: correlates and conundrums within and across cultures. *Social Science & Medicine, 45*(8), 1161–1176. https://doi.org/10.1016/S0277-9536(97)00022-1

Friedman, S. H., & Resnick, P. J. (2007). Child murder by mothers: patterns and prevention. *World Psychiatry, 6*(3), 137. https://www.ncbi.nlm.nih.gov/pmc/articles/PMC2174580/

Gul, P., Cross, S. E., & Uskul, A. K. (2021). Implications of culture of honor theory and research for practitioners and prevention researchers. *American Psychologist, 76*(3), 502–515. https://doi.org/10.1037/amp0000653

Hayes, B. E., Freilich, J. D., & Chermak, S. M. (2016). An exploratory study of honor crimes in the United States. *Journal of Family Violence, 31*, 303–314. https://doi.org/10.1007/s10896-016-9801-7

Idriss, M. M. (Ed.). (2020). *Men, masculinities, and honour-based abuse*. Routledge.

Idriss, M. M. (2022). Abused by the patriarchy: Male victims, masculinity, "honor"-based abuse and forced marriages. *Journal of Interpersonal Violence, 37*(13–14), NP11905–NP11932. https://doi.org/10.1177/0886260521997928

Irfan, S., & Cowburn, M. (2004). Disciplining, chastisement, and physical child abuse: perceptions and attitudes of the British Pakistani community. *Journal of Muslim minority affairs, 24*(1), 89–98. https://doi.org/10.1080/1360200042000212151

Janssen, J., Sanberg, R., & van der Sluis, D. (2011). Virtual honour: violating and restoring family honour through the Internet. In E. De Pauw, P. Ponsaers, K. van der Vijver, W. Bruggeman, & P. Deelman (Eds.). *Technology-led policing* (vol. 3, pp. 275–294). Maklu.

Jha, S. (2023, August 12). Man 'kills daughter and parades body on motorbike' for leaving home for two days. *ITV News*. https://www.itv.com/news/2023-08-12/man-kills-daughter-and-parades-body-on-motorbike-for-leaving-home-for-two-days?utm_medium=Social&utm_source=Twitter#Echobox=1691837154

Kandiyoti, D. (1988). Bargaining with patriarchy. *Gender & Society, 2*(3), 274–290. https://doi.org/10.1177/089124388002003004

Kaur, R. N. (2018). *'Call It What You Like, But… This Is Different': Exploring How Domestic Abuse Practitioners Understand and Address' Honour'-Based Violence* (Doctoral dissertation, The University of Manchester, UK). https://www.proquest.com/dissertations-theses/call-what-you-like-this-is-different-exploring/docview/2548915884/se-2

Khan, R. (2017). Sibling violence: Validating a two-factor model of severity in nonoffender populations. *Psychology of Violence, 7*(4), 498. http://dx.doi.org/10.1037/vio0000067

Khan, R. (2018a). Introduction to the special issue on honour-based abuse, violence and killings. *Journal of Aggression, Conflict and Peace Research, 10*(4), 237–238. https://doi.org/10.1108/JACPR-10-2018-360

Khan, R. (2018b). Attitudes towards "honor" violence and killings in collectivist cultures: Gender differences in Middle Eastern, North African, South Asian (MENASA) and Turkish populations. In J. L. Ireland, P. Birch, & C. A. Ireland (Eds.), *International Handbook in Aggression: Current Issues and Perspectives* (pp. 216–226). Routledge. https://doi.org/10.4324/9781315618777

Khan, R. & Brewer, G. (2021). Financial abuse and control of siblings. In Todd K. Shackelford (Ed.), *SAGE Handbook of Domestic Violence* (pp. 794–808). SAGE. http://digital.casalini.it/9781529742329

Khan, R., Morris, P., & Mulongo, P. (2024). *So-called 'honour' based abuse, forced marriage, and female genital mutilation in Greater Manchester. Scoping and research exercise.* Greater Manchester Combined Authority. https://www.greatermanchester-ca.gov.uk/

Khan, R., & Rogers, P. (2015). The normalization of sibling violence: Does gender and personal experience of violence influence perceptions of physical assault against siblings? *Journal of Interpersonal Violence, 30*(3), 437–458. https://doi.org/10.1177/0886260514535095

Khan, R., Saleem, S., & Lowe, M. (2018). "Honour"-based violence in a British South Asian community. *Safer Communities, 17*(1), 11–21. https://doi.org/10.1108/SC-02-2017-0007

Kizilhan, J. I. (2019). The impact of culture and belief in so-called honour killings a comparative study between honour murders and other perpetrators of violence in Germany. *Journal of Forensic Investigation, 7*(1), 1–7. https://www.dhbw-vs.de/files/content/03_FORSCHUNG/TCultHS/Publikationen/Papers/2019-09-03-Honour-killings-JFI-2330-0396-07-0043.pdf

Kulwicki, A. D. (2002). The practice of honor crimes: A glimpse of domestic violence in the Arab world. *Issues in Mental Health Nursing, 23*(1), 77–87. https://doi.org/10.1080/01612840252825491

Lowe, M., Khan, R., Thanzami, V., Barzy, M., & Karmaliani, R. (2021). Anti-gay "honor" abuse: A multinational attitudinal study of collectivist-versus individualist-orientated populations in Asia and England. *Journal of Interpersonal Violence, 36*(15–16), 7866–7885. https://doi.org/10.1177/0886260519838493

Mahapatra, N., & Murugan, V. (2024). South Asian young adults and gender roles: expectations, expressions, and intimate partner violence prevention. *Violence against Women, 30*(6–7), 1614–1633. https://doi.org/10.1177/10778012231156155

Naz, R v England and Wales Court of Appeal (Criminal Division). (2000, May 23). https://www.casemine.com/judgement/uk/5a938b3f60d03e5f6b82bbfc#

Oberwittler, D., & Kasselt, J. (2014). Honor Killings. In R. Gartner, & B. McCarthy (Eds.), *The Oxford Handbook of Gender, Sex, and Crime* (pp. 652–670). Oxford University Press. https://doi.org/10.1093/oxfordhb/9780199838707.013.0033

Office for National Statistics. (2023). *Domestic abuse victim characteristics, England and Wales: year ending March 2023.* https://www.ons.gov.uk/peoplepopulationandcommunity/crimeandjustice/articles/domesticabusevictimcharacteristicsenglandandwales/yearendingmarch2023#domestic-homicide

Onal, A. (2012). *Honour killing: Stories of men who killed.* Saqi Books.

Osterman, L. L., & Brown, R. P. (2011). Culture of Honor and Violence Against the Self. *Personality and Social Psychology Bulletin, 37*(12), 1611–1623. https://doi.org/10.1177/0146167211418529

Perkins, N. H., & Rai, A. (2023). Physical and Emotional Sibling Violence Among South Asian Immigrants in the United States. *Journal of Family Violence,* 1–13. https://doi.org/10.1007/s10896-023-00493-y

Pocock, M., Jackson, D., & Bradbury-Jones, C. (2020). Intimate partner violence and the power of love: A qualitative systematic review. *Health Care for Women International, 41*(6), 621–646. https://doi.org/10.1080/07399332.2019.1621318

Purkayastha, B. (2000). Liminal lives: South Asian youth and domestic violence. *Journal of Social Distress and the Homeless, 9*(3), 201–219. https://doi.org/10.1023/A:1009408018107

Qandeel Baloch: Court acquits brother of Pakistan star's murder. (2022, February 15). BBC News. https://www.bbc.co.uk/news/world-asia-60388111

Regis-Moura, A., Ferreira, L. B., Bonfá-Araujo, B., & Iglesias, F. (2022). "If not Mine, She Won't Belong to Another": Mechanisms of Moral Disengagement in a Femicide Perpetrator from Brazil. *Violence Against Women, 28*(12–13), 3135–3153. https://doi.org/10.1177/10778012211038969

Relva, I. & Khan, R. (2021). Siblicide: The Psychology of Sibling Homicide. In R. Geffner, J. W. White, L. K. Hamberger, A. Rosenbaum, V. Vaughan-Eden, & V. I. Vieth (Eds) (2021). *Handbook of interpersonal violence and abuse across the lifespan: A project of the National Partnership to End Interpersonal Violence Across the Lifespan* (pp. 1323–1341). Springer. https://doi.org/10.1007/978-3-319-89999-2_288

Resnick, P. J. (2016). Filicide in the United States. *Indian Journal of Psychiatry, 58*(2), S203–S209. https://doi.org/10.4103/0019-5545.196845

Salter, M. (2014). Multi-perpetrator domestic violence. *Trauma, Violence, & Abuse, 15*(2), 102–112. https://doi.org/10.1177/1524838013511542

Sandhu, K. K., & Barrett, H. (2024). Girls just wanna have fun! South Asian women in the UK diaspora: Gradations of choice, agency, consent, and coercion. *Wome's Studies International Forum, 102*, 102859. https://doi.org/10.1016/j.wsif.2023.102859

Sandhu, K. K., & Barrett, H. R. (2020). "Should I stay, or should I go?": the experiences of, and choices available to women of south Asian heritage living in the UK when leaving a relationship of choice following intimate partner violence (IPV). *Social Sciences, 9*(9), 151. https://doi.org/10.3390/socsci9090151

Shahbazi, H., Sadeghi, M. A., & Panaghi, L. (2023). Dehumanization in female victims of intimate partner violence. *Journal of Injury & Violence Research, 15*(1), 83–95. https://doi.org/10.5249/jivr.v15i1.1676

Singh, D., & Bhandari, D. S. (2021). Legacy of honor and violence: an analysis of factors responsible for honor killings in Afghanistan, Canada, India, and Pakistan as Discussed in Selected Documentaries on Real Cases. *SAGE Open, 11*(2). https://doi.org/10.1177/21582440211022323

Smith, D. L. (2011). *Less than human: Why we demean, enslave, and exterminate others.* St. Martin's Press.

Solarino, B., Punzi, G., Di Vella, G., Carabellese, F., & Catanesi, R. (2019). A multidisciplinary approach in overkill: Analysis of 13 cases and review of the literature. *Forensic Science International, 298*, 402–407. https://doi.org/10.1016/j.forsciint.2019.03.029

Statista Research Department. (2023a, June 2). *Number of perpetrators in child abuse cases in the United States in 2021, by relationship to victim.* https://www.statista.com/statistics/418484/number-of-perpetrators-in-child-abuse-cases-in-the-us-by-relationship-to-victim/

Statista Research Department. (2023b, June 2). *Number of perpetrators in child abuse cases in the United States in 2021, by sex.* https://www.statista.com/statistics/418470/number-of-perpetrators-in-child-abuse-cases-in-the-us-by-sex/

Stead, L., Brewer, G., Gardner, K., & Khan, R. (2022). Sexual coercion perpetration and victimisation in females: The influence of borderline and histrionic personality traits, rejection sensitivity, and love styles. *Journal of Sexual Aggression, 28*(1), 15–27. https://doi.org/10.1080/13552600.2021.1909156

van Baak, C., Hayes, B. E., Freilich, J. D., & Chermak, S. M. (2018). Honor Crimes in the United States and Offenders' Neutralization Techniques. *Deviant Behavior, 39*(2), 187–202. https://doi.org/10.1080/01639625.2016.1266870

Vandello, J. (2016). Do we need a psychology of women in the Islamic world? *Sex Roles, 75*, 623–629. https://doi.org/10.1007/s11199-016-0691-1

Walsh, J. A., & Krienert, J. L. (2014). My brother's reaper: Examining officially reported siblicide incidents in the United States, 2000–2007. *Violence & Victims, 29*(3), 523–540. https://doi.org/10.1891/0886-6708.VV-D-13-00032

Way, N., & Rogers, L. O. (2017). Resistance to dehumanization during childhood and adolescence: A developmental and contextual process. In N. Budwig, E. Turil, & P. D. Zelazo (Eds.), *New perspectives on Human Development* (pp. 229–225). Cambridge University Press.

Wolfgang, M. E. (1958). *Patterns in criminal homicide.* University of Pennsylvania Press.

World Health Organization. (2021). *Violence against women prevalence estimates, 2018.* https://iris.who.int/bitstream/handle/10665/341337/9789240022256-eng.pdf?sequence=1

Wren, B., Launer, J., Music, G., Reiss, M. J., & Swanepoel, A. (2021). Can an evolutionary perspective shed light on maternal abuse of children?. *Clinical Child psychology and Psychiatry, 26*(1), 283–294. https://uk.sagepub.com/en-gb/journals-permissions

Conclusions

7

This book has been written with the knowledge that psychology has a crucial part to play in understanding and responding to "honor" abuse, violence, and killings. Indeed, this book is a determined effort to provide much-needed nuance to the dominant Eurocentric discourse in family violence, child abuse, and domestic homicide in forensic psychology and related criminal justice fields. The underlying theme running through this book, linking each chapter to the next, is the fact that 21st-century psychology teaching and research have been shaped by historical legacies of racism. Racial bias is not a small stain on the periphery of current psychology. It is sewn into the very fabric of traditional methods and theories on human cognition, emotion, and behavior and underpins the formulation of new research questions, research design, data analysis and interpretation, and conclusion formulation. The chapters in this book have illustrated that Western academic psychology is still "raceless" and that "honor" abuse, violence, and killings are a blind spot in family violence, child abuse, and domestic homicide literature.

Each chapter in this book has dramatic implications for researchers and practitioners on how to work compassionately with victims and understand the behavior of perpetrators of "honor" abuse, violence, and killings. This book is also a call to action for research to evolve beyond simple, unsophisticated, and broad cross-cultural comparisons using unreliable fuzzy data and racial stereotypes and instead advance by exploring the influence of cognitive, emotional, behavioral, and social factors as antecedents to "honor" abuse, violence and killing. It is also necessary to recognize that established theories and traditional perspectives often do not apply to victims and perpetrators who have minoritized racial and ethnic identities.

DOI: 10.4324/9781003299950-9

A core tenet of this book is the rejection of simple explanations for "honor" abuse, violence, and killings. As all the evidence points to a reality that is far more complex, single-factor explanations that focus solely on culture or religion are easy, convenient, and lazy.

This chapter ends with a reminder that behind every crime statistic is a history of trauma and a legacy of grief. To bring this book to a close, the final words have been written by Shaheen Hashmat, a survivor of "honor" abuse and forced marriage.

As someone with lived experience of "honor" abuse, I was fortunate to have escaped my situation at 12 years old. But after a suicide attempt at 13, I spent years in and out of therapy and was repeatedly, seriously failed by mental health practitioners who had no idea what to do with me. How I wish they had access to this book.

Dr Khan's work highlights the interplay between foundational gaps in psychology research and reductive perceptions of victims that lead to persistent dehumanization. By providing a fuller picture of the drivers and impacts of "honor" abuse, violence, and killings while accounting for psychosocial factors, Dr Khan challenges predominantly WEIRD-informed practitioners to see racialized victims as people instead of the sum of their stereotyped identities. In my own memoir, *It Ends With Us*, I have also been guided to challenge the critical voice that still tells me I am nothing more than my family's shame. Finding parts of my authentic self under the rubble of a dozen labels that have been forced onto me has been a painful process.

Throughout my time as an independent campaigner against forced marriage and "honor" based abuse, I shared my story many times. Sadly, on most occasions, I felt like little more than the subject of passing anthropological interest. As a psychotherapy client, I felt alienated. I know I am not alone in these experiences. This book signals a profound change in the way we understand "honor" abuse, violence, and killings.

I am hopeful for my sisters- and brothers-in-arms who are fighting to survive. We are worth knowing.

Index

Note: Pages in **bold** refer to tables.

T - #0014 - 011124 - C0 - 234/156/9 - PB - 9781032290812 - Matt Lamination